D0436201

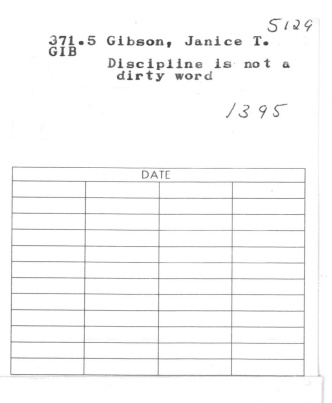

DATE			

Discipline
IS Not
A DirtyWord

Discipline IS Not A Dirty Word

A Positive Learning Approach

5 / 29

JANICE T. GIBSON, Ed.D.

The Lewis Publishing Company
Lexington, Massachusetts
Brattleboro, Vermont

This book is manufactured in the United States of America. It is
published by The Lewis Publishing Company,
Fessenden Road, Brattleboro, Vermont 05301.

Library of Congress Cataloging in Publication Data

Gibson, Janice T.
  Discipline is not a dirty word.

Bibliography.
Includes index.
1. School discipline. 2. Learning, Psychology of.
3. Behavior modification. 4. Cognition in children.
5. Child rearing. 6. Parenting.   I. Title.
LB3012.G5 1983   371.5   83–1010
ISBN 0–86616–027–2
ISBN 0–86616–023–X (pbk.)

PUBLISHED MARCH 1983
Second printing October 1983

Contents

Discipline
IS Not
A Dirty Word

PART I

DON'T BE AFRAID TO DISCIPLINE

CHAPTER 1

What Is Discipline All About?

The new family on the block is happy and prosperous. The parents, Ann and Bob Lewis, are warm and friendly. They keep their house looking inviting: the lawn is well groomed and from late spring until fall there are cheery red geraniums blooming in the windows. But it is the Lewis children who have really impressed the neighbors. They are happy, exuberant, and playful. They seem to enjoy everything they do and they always seem to be doing something. In the summer months and on weekends, neighbors can hear the sounds of their laughter at all times of day coming from the gameroom or backyard where they are at play.

Ten-year-old David and eight-year-old Carrie are friendly and outgoing. It took them only a short time after they moved into the neighborhood to make a large number of friends. Other children enjoy their company and, because they feel comfortable at the Lewis home, tend to congregate there for play.

Adults also enjoy the Lewis children. The youngsters have been taught how to interact with people of all ages and can chat comfortably with grownups without feeling awkward or shy. The neighbors are delighted with them.

What has led to this happy state of affairs? Is it sheer luck or have Bob and Ann done something special? Parents of other children who play regularly with the Lewis kids think that one reason these children are so popular is that they are very well disciplined. In fact, Bob and Ann have taught them specific ways to behave that make it enjoyable for others to be around them.

3

Is discipline the key to the Lewis family's success?

"It's true we set down rules of behavior for our kids," agrees Bob Lewis. "And Davie and Carrie are obedient children. But Ann and I aren't what you'd call strict disciplinarians. In fact, we almost never punish our kids. I think I can count on one hand the number of times that I remember."

In point of fact, Bob and Ann almost never resort to punishment. But then, it's extremely unusual for either of the children to do anything really bad because Bob and Ann have disciplined so effectively.

What does it mean to discipline effectively? Many parents who have talked with me seem to think of discipline itself almost as a type of punishment. One mother who came into my office, for example, reported that she wished her eleven-year-old son were more like Davie Lewis. She was determined to discipline him well. The last time she had disciplined him, she told me, she had washed his mouth out with soap.

"I let the punishment fit the crime," she said.

What was the crime?

"Swearing like a trooper. It was the first time he had used language like that around me, and I was determined it would be the last time. He had a good lesson."

This mother thought her behavior was that of a good disciplinarian. In fact, she was a very ineffective one. The very next day her son cursed his mother once again. Clearly, punishment of the sort meted out by this mother and under the conditions of this learning situation simply didn't accomplish what she wanted.

Although many people, like this mother, assume that a good disciplinarian metes out punishment regularly, to discipline, by definition, does not mean to punish at all (though in some situations punishment may aid in the discipline process). Nor does it mean to ignore bad behavior. The verb "to discipline," according to Webster's dictionary, means to "train by instruction," in other words, simply "to teach." Using this definition, an effective disciplinarian is first and foremost a good teacher. Bob and Ann Lewis were effective disciplinarians because they taught their children what they wanted them to do, to act in ways that made it easy for them to get along with others and with themselves. In doing so, they implicitly taught them how not to behave. It was precisely because they were so successful at this latter teaching task that the Lewises almost never resorted to punishment.

Teaching—and learning—how and how not to act is what discipline is all about. Parents who understand this fact and make the best use of the principles of teaching and learning are most likely to be, like the Lewises, successful at their job of child-rearing.

A PRACTICAL APPROACH TO DISCIPLINE

Discipline Is Not a Dirty Word takes a practical approach to the problem of disciplining children in America today. It examines closely what works—and why. As a psychologist who has worked with children from a variety of cultural backgrounds and a parent of two children who have grown up in America, I have spent a large portion of the past twenty-five years closely involved with both successful and unsuccessful discipline. As a research psychologist, I have studied discipline in a variety of cultural settings and the effects of different types of discipline on the personal and social development of children. As a mother, I have studied in a far more intimate manner discipline and its effects on children in a variety of personal and social settings.

In *Discipline Is Not a Dirty Word* I have described those discipline methods that are most effective in teaching children how to interact successfully in the worlds in which they are growing up. These methods are described in terms of the two basic approaches mentioned above: that of a parent concerned with what works and what doesn't work and that of a psychologist concerned with why.

Discipline is one of the most important aspects of child-rearing, and parents who are successful disciplinarians are likely to have the happiest, most well-adjusted children. Parents who misunderstand the process and treat discipline solely as a form of punishment, and parents who, conversely, are afraid of discipline or who believe that the best way to raise children is to let them grow up by themselves are more likely to have children who don't learn or who learn the wrong things. Children do not learn from punishment alone. At best, they would be unhappy children. Neither do they learn without instruction. Learning, after all, doesn't take place in a vacuum: without parents or other important adults to provide the teaching, children are likely to learn different lessons from whomever or whatever happens to be around.

Discipline Is Not a Dirty Word takes an eclectic approach to methods of child-rearing and discipline. That is, it doesn't take a single viewpoint, but uses the best aspects of all positions. As a parent, I have always found this approach useful: I cared less whether my child-rearing methods would have been acceptable to Sigmund Freud or B.F. Skinner or Benjamin Spock than whether they helped my children become what I wanted: happy, healthy, well-adjusted youngsters. As a psychologist, I also believe that the many different situations in which parents find themselves require flexibility and that no one approach taken by researchers has yet solved all the problems facing parents. Sigmund Freud, for example, was not faced with the realities of the 1980s and therefore did not develop specific approaches to deal with them. B.F. Skinner never addressed himself to the question of how to provide the love, warmth, and affection necessary for the development of self-esteem. Benjamin Spock (not a psychologist) has presented a practical approach and has dealt with the issues related to changing times and the importance of love, warmth, and affection as well as the effects of rewards and punishments on children's behavior. He hasn't, however, dealt with these issues in a variety of microcultural and cultural situations important to many children growing up today. Just as no one child-rearing situation is exactly like another (we grow up with different viewpoints, interests in children, and facilities for child-rearing), and no one set of parents and children has the same life experiences as any other, no one approach alone can solve all problems.

The multiple approaches to discipline described in this book do work—when they are used carefully with one another, and when they form the basis of a full-time child-rearing project. Disciplining, like all other aspects of child-rearing, must be a full-time job to be effective. This is not to say that a parent needs to be with a child twenty-four hours a day to be successful. Working parents have demonstrated that they can raise their children as successfully as parents who remain at home—so long as they ensure that the disciplining methods used by their surrogates in their absence are consistent with the methods that they themselves practice.

Successful disciplining requires full-time teachers—parents or surrogates who show children by their own actions what is good and not good to do. It requires consistent rewarding of good behavior—so that children learn that good behavior is useful to them—and care to ensure that bad behavior doesn't get rewarded. It requires love, warmth, and caring—all of the time, not just when it's easy for us to give.

THREE IMPORTANT PRINCIPLES TO KEEP IN MIND WHILE READING

Teaching Good Behavior Is Easiest When You Are a Good Model Yourself

Children learn a great deal about how to behave simply by observing and imitating what they see. Because parents usually spend more time with their children than do any other adults, most of what children do, particularly in their early years, is learned from watching their parents. Children, who get a great deal of pleasure from being as much like their parents as they can, first imitate their parents' actions and then gradually come to feel about those behaviors the same as they think their parents feel about them. For example, children whose parents spend a lot of time at home reading or listening to music are likely to read and listen to music a lot themselves—and like it. Conversely, children whose parents spend all their free evening hours glued to the TV set are likely to watch TV as much as they can.

Similarly, the mother who is meticulous about her appearance and who enjoys being complimented on her clothes is far more likely to have a child who tries to stay neat, clean, and attractive—and who likes clothes—than a mother who is sloppy and shows no interest in her appearance. Parents who cheat on their income tax and proudly tell the family that they will all go on a fun vacation

with the proceeds shouldn't be surprised if their children begin to
develop their own ways of cheating to get different rewards.

The message from all this to parents? Parents who want their
children to act in certain ways need to be models of those ways
themselves—something that is often difficult but nevertheless is one
of the most important lessons in good discipline.

Children Learn What Is and What Is Not Worthwhile to Them and Behave Accordingly

Children are great pragmatists. A great deal of what they learn is
devoted to finding out just what they can do to get themselves what
they want—whether this is social approval, knowledge that they can
do something really well, the joy of discovering knowledge, or simply some kind of material reward. They are far more likely to continue to behave in ways that get them what they want than in ways
that don't. The father of the small girl who sorely wants his attention
and approval who praises her whenever she uses proper table manners is going far to develop good manners in his child. If the same
father ignores this child except to punish her when she's sloppy at
the table, he will have far less success. His daughter won't want
nearly as much to learn good manners because they never get her
what she wants.

Children are very quick to learn when behaving in a certain way
will be worthwhile to them and when it will not. For this reason,
parents who are careful not to reward bad behaviors can help their
children stop being bad. However, if they are careful not to reward
bad behavior only in situations where it is easy to ignore this behavior, their children are likely to learn how to manipulate the
situation to their advantage. For example, if parents effectively
control their children's tantrums at home by carefully ignoring them
but give in when other people are around in order to avoid the
embarrassment, their children will learn very quickly to throw tantrums in public.

The message in this instance is clear: parents need to reward the
actions they want carefully and consistently, and to ensure that
behavior they don't want never gets rewarded equally carefully and
consistently.

Lots of Love, Warmth, and Affection Makes Learning Anything Easier—and Fun, Too

Being a good model and rewarding good behavior are important principles of good discipline. By themselves, however, they aren't enough. The best modeling behavior and the most consistent rewards may be ineffective if parents fail to satisfy their children's emotional needs. Children need lots of love, warmth, and affection; psychologists suggest that when these needs are met, children learn more easily. When they aren't met, children are so busy trying to satisfy them that they often have too little time or interest to learn what their parents want.

In other words, parents need to love their children and to show them this love in observable ways. If they do, their children will want to learn and will learn easily. For parents who are affectionate and outgoing, this is easy as well as fun. For parents who find it more difficult to let their children know their good feelings this can sometimes create problems. But these are not insurmountable. Parents need to learn how to express their own feelings and communicate freely their own emotional states to their children. In this way, they can teach their children to communicate freely in return and to let their parents know and understand their needs. The cold, distant parent who takes the position that children should obey and be seen and not heard will have far more difficulty in getting what he or she wants than the parent who learns to be available as a friend and companion, who is there to listen when needed, and who understands and remembers what it was like to be a child. The parent who learns this lesson is likely to have a child who feels worthwhile.[1]

SOME THOUGHTS ON WHAT WE SHOULD BE TEACHING OUR CHILDREN

So far, I have made two major points in relation to discipline. The first is that effective disciplinarians are good teachers. The second is that there are a number of basic principles we should adhere to in order to be good teachers. But if you want to be a good disciplinarian, you must do one more thing, which sounds far easier than it often is: you must decide what behavior you want to teach. More specifically, you must decide precisely which behaviors you want to encourage and which you want to stop.

The answer to the question of what constitutes "good" and "bad" behavior, at least in our own culture, is a personal one. Often parents disagree strongly on specific behaviors they label "good" or "bad." Take gum-chewing, for example. This is a behavior many parents consider revolting. Many other parents enjoy chewing gum themselves and happily give it to their children.

Another behavior considered valuable by some parents and ignored by others is studying a musical instrument. Parents who believe that one of the most important skills a child can develop is playing a musical instrument usually want their children to develop the habit of practicing daily. Parents who don't care about music themselves or who aren't interested in whether their children can play an instrument are not interested at all in practicing.

Although parents may disagree about specific behaviors they want to foster, most agree on a general type of behavior that they believe important. Children growing up in our culture need to learn to act in a variety of ways that will help them get along with other people and adjust to the world in which they live.

Getting along with others and being popular tend to be characteristics that are valued in our society. Bob and Ann Lewis believe that these particular attributes require some specific skills, and they carefully set out to teach them. They taught their children the abilities to share, to engage in conversation with people of all ages, and, because Bob Lewis's job requires the family to move from city to city, to introduce themselves easily to prospective new playmates. They taught their children, in addition, how to act in ways that are not self-destructive or destructive to others. Davie and Carrie learned, for example, not to act aggressively at play and to take care of and not destroy possessions. They also learned how to act in school in ways that pleased their teachers and that made it easier for them to learn academic skills: they came to class on time, paid attention, and tackled school problems with vigor and interest. All of these behaviors will help Davie and Carrie grow up to be socially acceptable, well-adjusted, and responsible young adults. They are all behaviors that most American parents would like to foster in their children and with which *Discipline Is Not a Dirty Word* deals in subsequent chapters.

Of course, not all behaviors are this easy to categorize, which is often where the problem comes in. A pitfall for some parents is that sometimes it's simply hard to decide what's "good" or "bad." Another is that sometimes parents decide that certain behaviors are bad because they are annoying, even when they actually lead to good adjustment for their children. In this case, the parents may teach children to stop behaviors that actually are good for them.

One common example is creative behavior. Sometimes creative behavior that involves inventiveness, flexibility, and constructiveness is considered bad by parents because it is noisy or makes a mess. A good example is the child who is learning how to paint, and in his zeal at creation accidentally spills his poster paints on the floor. The parent who is more concerned that the child remain neat rather than interested in what he is attempting to create might teach him to stop this behavior, thus reducing future attempts at creativity. Another example is the child who gets extremely excited about what she is learning and wants a great deal of attention and help. This child is likely to appear annoying to a tired parent who just wants to come home and rest after work. Creativity, of course, can be fostered by good discipline—when parents are careful to reward creative acts with their interest and encouragement.

Child psychologists have studied attitudes of parents and teachers toward what they considered to be good and bad behaviors and have noted that many adults are bothered by very noisy activity or simply by children asking too many questions. For these parents and teachers, "good" behavior often involves keeping quiet, being still, and being docile.[2] But what does fostering docile behavior mean for children? Certainly not good adjustment to the world in which they are going to live! We may think that a quiet, docile child is cute. An adult who is going to be successful in the world, however, needs to have learned to express some exuberance. A quiet, docile adult is usually considered boring, not cute; we are likely to do our best to avoid an adult who has learned the lesson of docility too well.

The message here is simple: when you choose behaviors to encourage and discourage, examine them carefully. Make sure you know why you are choosing them and that what you teach your children is to their advantage!

Another important factor for you to consider is whether or not what you are asking is something your child can do. Age and, more importantly, developmental level are the crucial issues here. Too many parents try to teach their children specific skills that are beyond their developmental level. When the children don't learn, these parents often look unsuccessfully to other methods of discipline. However, there are many skills we can't teach successfully by any method until our children have reached the necessary level of development or have acquired the necessary prerequisite skills.

Often something we can't teach our child no matter what we do becomes a simple task if we just wait awhile. For example, although we can teach two-year-olds to play side by side with other children, we can't teach them to share no matter how hard we try. We can, however, do so a year or two later. Four-year-old children can learn not only to share but also to accept help from a playmate in a game and to play cooperative games, for example—skills that the two-year-old can't possibly learn. Parents can easily teach five-year-olds to put away their toys. They have to wait until their children are far more mature, however, to teach them successfully to help around the house in more complex ways, for example, taking responsibility for sorting laundry or cooking.

Another point that needs to be made is that parents, when deciding what behaviors to encourage, need to realize that a great deal of child behavior is neither good nor bad, but is simply normal. Many age-related behaviors suddenly appear one day and go away the next, and parents don't need to do anything about them. Many of these are annoying to us but don't really hurt anybody. A good example is the four-year-old who suddenly develops a new habit of saying "No!" to everything asked of her. She even says "No!" while doing what she is supposed to do! Four-year-old verbal negativism can drive tired parents to distraction, but it usually has hardly any effect on the rest of the child's behavior. If we just wait, this behavior will go away—most probably before the child's next birthday.

Older children also exhibit normal behaviors that many parents may need to learn to live with. Children who scream, make lots of noise, and act in boisterous ways can bother parents and other adults who are used to peace and quiet. Noise is, however, a normal part of growing up for many children. And it, too, often goes away as children get older.

The teenage habit of talking for hours on the telephone about nothing is another example of an annoying but relatively harmless age-related behavior. Teenagers need to stop talking on the telephone if it affects their school grades adversely or if other people in the household are inconvenienced. Otherwise, "telephonitis" is an age-related adolescent disease that usually goes away by itself with the passing of adolescence.

It is important to distinguish between these annoying but harmless normal behaviors and bad behaviors. The best way to deal with normal but harmless behaviors is to learn to live with them. There are so many things that children need to learn in the course of growing up and that parents need to teach that parents only make learning more difficult if they try to teach too many things at one time. Children need to have some freedom to do some normal things. The best that we as parents can do is learn to adjust as much as possible to the conditions they present and wait for the behaviors to go away.

Finally, there are many things that children do in the course of growing up that can be self-destructive or destructive to others. These are the bad behaviors that parents should do their best to stop. Most American parents living in cities, for example, would agree that we need to teach our young children that they can't run in the street. In a similar vein, we need to teach them that they can't bite, hit, or attack other children. They also can't destroy the property of other people. As they get older, we need to teach them that they can't insult or offend other people. When parents ask their teenage children in a reasonable way to do something, such as help with the dishes, and there is no objective reason for refusing, teen-agers must learn that they shouldn't simply and rudely refuse. This behavior doesn't lead to adult acceptance of adult responsibility. The successful parent-teacher includes getting rid of this type of behavior as part of necessary discipline.

THE RECORD SO FAR

In a number of research projects I have conducted together with graduate students in my psychology classes, strangers on the streets were polled and asked what they thought was the most serious problem facing American parents today. Some of our respondents were parents themselves. Others were children themselves or adults with no children. The response by more than half of each group polled was that "American parents don't do enough to discipline their children. They don't know how anymore." Parents, teachers, and other watchers of children agreed that children "simply don't behave the way we want them to."

The evidence backs up the views of these respondents: children often don't get along with their parents, teachers, or peers. They often don't try hard enough to learn in school. Some children vandalize school property and use alcohol or drugs indiscriminately. Teenage sexual activity is on the rise. Police report increased crime. As we entered the 1980s, 73 percent of the nation's schools were reporting more than one serious crime a semester; more crimes were being committed by children and adolescents than by adults. Even serious depressive behavior among children is on the increase, according to researchers.[3]

All of these situations represent examples of children learning bad ways of behaving instead of ways that lead to social adjustment and eventually to responsible adult ways of acting.

Learning responsible ways of acting is rarely accomplished on the street or without consistent parental control. It begins at home—with good teaching and with parents who don't think that discipline is a dirty word!

**WHAT *DISCIPLINE IS NOT A DIRTY WORD*
PROVIDES PARENTS**

What you have read so far presents my views of what discipline means and how it can help you and your child. Subsequent parts of the book tell you how to discipline.

Part II provides practical approaches to discipline, making use of several schools of thought and points of view. Chapters 2–4 each present one position on how children learn and what parents can do about it. Three principles emerge from these positions: *Teaching good behavior is easiest when you are a good model yourself; Children learn what is and what is not worthwhile to them and behave accordingly; Lots of love, warmth, and affection makes learning anything easier and more fun, too.*

Chapter 5 provides specific rules to follow based on all these principles.

Part III describes special discipline cases as well as discipline problems in situations common in America today. Chapter 6, for example, deals with family situations in which it is not easy to discipline: when children and parents are dealing with divorce, when parents are trying to raise children by themselves and need to take on a variety of responsibilities they used to share with another parent, when remarriage creates stepparents and stepchildren and everyone in the new family unit needs to learn to adjust to one another, and when both parents work outside the home. Chapter 7 provides help for parents who feel they are losing control of adolescent children. This chapter deals with delinquent and pre-delinquent behaviors as well as adolescent sexual activity and depressive behavior. Chapter 8 is for parents who feel they have lost control of their discipline completely and are in danger of being or becoming abusing parents. This chapter explains why child abuse is on the increase and some ways that parents can begin solving the problem. All three chapters include rules to follow instead of letting panic set in.

Part IV contains information for parents who want additional help. It's often hard for a parent to tell whether an annoying behavior is bad and needs to be changed or is a normal age-related behavior that is just an annoyance. This portion of the book includes a chart describing age-related behaviors that will help you know what to expect from your child at various age levels between pre-school and high school and decide whether what you see your child doing should be expected or considered a problem behavior. Part IV also includes useful readings on child and adolescent development, child rearing, disciplining, and day care as well as a guide to services in your communities that can provide help and keep panic from setting in.

PART II

SOME APPROACHES TO DISCIPLINE THAT WORK

CHAPTER 2

Teaching Good Behavior Is Easiest When You Are a Good Model Yourself

Four-year-old Lucy was playing "house" with the little boy next door. "You be the Poppa and I'll be the Momma," she suggested. "First we'll eat supper, and then we go to bed. We both jump up and down on the bed for awhile, and then you get up and go to the bathroom, and get me a cigarette."

Lucy's mother was mortified in front of the neighbors.

"Wherever did the child pick that up?" she mumbled. "We moved to a bigger apartment so she could have her own bedroom a year ago!"

CHILDREN IMITATE WHAT THEY SEE AND HEAR

Lucy obviously picked up her information about what Momma and Poppa do from seeing and hearing. Our children observe—and imitate—far more of our behaviors than most of us realize. All during the days (and nights) that we are engaged in our own activities, our children are our silent observers. Most of what they imitate serves to increase their social skills. For example, Lucy learned how to speak in large part through imitating the sounds she heard her

19

parents make and then learning to attach meaning to them. She learned to eat with a spoon and then with a fork by watching her parents at the table and imitating what she saw them do.

Sometimes, however, if parents aren't careful, children's observations and imitation can lead them to behave in ways we don't want. Lucy, through her play activity, let the neighbors know what goes on in her parents' bedroom and embarrassed her mother. Little Sarah, playing the same game, let the neighbors in on other activities of her parents.

In Sarah's game, she announced to her playmate, "I'll be the Mommy and you be the Daddy. When you come in late, I'll yell, 'Not again, you sneak! You go off with that tramp and expect me to be sitting here with the kids just taking it! I won't put up with it.' "

Sarah is seven years old; we hope that when she is twenty-seven, she won't still be imitating her parents' marital strife in a more harmful way.

PARENTS ARE MODELS SEVEN DAYS A WEEK

Because mothers and fathers are most likely to be the people who take care of children from the time they're born, they are the ones who most often serve as models. Whether they realize it or not, parents are models twenty-four hours a day, seven days a week.

Children learn by watching and imitating their parents from earliest infancy. We used to think that newborns weren't able to perceive their environments very well, let alone learn complex behavior. Recently, however, psychologists have discovered that they can learn rather complex behaviors if they have the opportunity to observe them through a model. One recent study, for example, showed that newborns who watched their mothers stick out their tongues, open their mouths, or even flutter their eyelashes were able to copy these behaviors.[1]

Just as infants watch and imitate their mothers, older babies listen carefully to the sounds they hear people make around them, watch what they see people doing, and do their best to imitate. The young child who watches his mother bake bread in the kitchen will probably imitate bread-making in his play; the child whose mother spends most of her free time at home working on the manuscript of a novel is likely to play at typewriting instead.

Why do Children Imitate?

Babies observe and imitate their parents apparently because it's interesting and fun. Because newborn infants do imitate, many psychologists believe that imitation is an innate response that teaches skills necessary for survival. These psychologists think that imitation carries with it its own reward: it's fun for infants and children because it helps them control themselves and their environment just a little bit more.

A good example of the motivating force behind imitation is the seven- or eight-month-old baby who develops strong attachment feelings for her mother. One reason that babies of this age become so attached to Mother is that they are aware of her power: she can do all sorts of wonderful things, such as provide food when they're hungry or dry diapers when they're cold and wet. Since babies perceive this power, imitating any behavior that their mothers make probably gives them vicarious feelings of power and control.[2]

Older children imitate their parents for many of the same reasons. When four-year-old Lucy plays house and jumps up and down on the bed with her little friend, she thinks she's acting like a grown-up woman. Lucy's pleasure comes from feeling as if she were a grownup, and, equally important, as if she possessed grown-up powers. Teenage interest in driving cars is another example of the same thing: when sixteen-year-old Donald watches every move his parents make when they are operating the family car, he has a very specific purpose. He wants to be able to drive the car just like his parents do. Driving gives him a feeling of being an adult. Equally important, it gives him a chance to expand and control his environment in ways he could never do before.

WHAT MODELS TEACH

Children learn continually from models around them. Many behaviors that we used to think of as innate are, in fact, learned from observation and imitation. The sex-typed behavior characteristic of males and females in our society is a good example.

No one is surprised when boys act aggressively in school or are wildly active on the playground. These are behaviors that we expect of boys, just as we expect them to play with trucks. No one is surprised, either, when girls are neat and dainty or when they play with dolls. This is what girls are supposed to do. Boys aren't born tough and girls dainty, however. They behave in certain ways and choose certain games because that's what they've learned to do.

We teach children to act in "masculine" and "feminine" ways via two related processes. First, we reward girls for imitating their mothers (or other females) and boys for imitating their fathers (or other males). Second, mothers and fathers act as models and demonstrate the desired behavior. It's no accident that in traditional families in which mothers behave in stereotypic feminine ways, for instance, taking charge of house and kitchen and enjoying sewing and baking, their daughters grow up doing the same thing. In a similar vein, in families in which fathers are stereotypically masculine, enjoying roughhousing, playing men's games, and disliking housework, sons usually grow up acting and feeling very much like their fathers.

In many modern families today in which mothers and fathers share and take on each other's traditional roles at home and on the job, children grow up with far fewer stereotypic sex-role identifications. Children who watch their mothers go off to the office every day or their fathers cook and do the dishes are not likely to think of women as dainty creatures who take care of hearth and home and men as tough creatures whose primary role is breadwinner. They also aren't likely to behave as if they do.

Sex-typed behavior is learned largely from imitating parents. But it isn't simply particular behaviors that are imitated; it's also the general attitudes that parents have toward sex roles. The child who watches a mother stay at home and play a very traditional housewife role and a father who sees himself primarily as the breadwinner who brings home the bacon is likely to have very different views of what to study in school, how to select friends, what clothes are appropriate, and what play activities are the most fun from a child who comes from a more modern family.

Parental sexual activities, as well as sex-typed behavior such as being tough or dainty, are often imitated by children. Parents who make it clear by their own behavior that it's all right to behave in sexually provocative ways are likely to have children who feel free to explore sexually themselves. This can be a major problem for single parents who, at the same time they're bringing up children, want (and need) to have their own sexual and social lives. What should parents do?

"Do as I say, not as I do" doesn't work in this situation. The single mother who has her boyfriend spend the weekend regularly and share her bedroom can expect her fourteen-year-old daughter to emulate her sexual behavior—if not with her mother's knowledge, then without it. One solution for single parents who don't want this to happen is to keep their sexual activities away from the house.

Children imitate specific behaviors. They also imitate broad styles of living. The child whose parents entertain socially a great deal may not want to entertain in exactly the same fashion herself. She may, however, become used to having a lot of people around and feel comfortable in a home where people enjoy coming to be entertained. The child whose parents enjoy serving as gracious hosts may be likely to enjoy having her own playmates over for the afternoon or having a pajama party instead.

Parents may also serve as models for certain styles of problem-solving. For example, parents who keep a large dictionary available so that they can look up new words as they run across them and who use it frequently are likely to have children who learn to look up answers when they have questions. These children are also likely to have vocabularies far more extensive than children who don't have models to teach them how to learn about language.

Problem-solving behavior, like many other behaviors, is learned from watching models in a variety of day-to-day situations. Parents aren't always aware that children are observing and imitating. As we noted before, it is for this reason that they sometimes find their children imitating behaviors they didn't mean to teach.

Most parents do their best not to model bad behaviors but to be the best models they can for good behaviors. Following are some descriptions of how to do this.

Good Behavior

Parents can teach good behavior both by demonstrating brand new ways to act and by showing children how to improve old behaviors.

Demonstrating Brand New Ways to Act. Parents serve as models for many behaviors that children might never have thought of if they hadn't first watched their parents. The father who obviously loves playing the violin, practices every evening after dinner, and regularly invites friends to come over to play quartet music is likely to have a child who wants to learn to play too. Because the child has had plenty of opportunity to learn just what a violinist needs to do in order to become good, he is far more likely to practice. In a similar vein, the mother who is able to complete law school, sets up a private practice, and clearly loves every minute of what she is doing professionally increases the probability that her daughters, by watching the steps she has gone through, will develop similar ways to be successful at their own careers.

The brand new behaviors in these examples both involve long-term practice. Every day, however, children are learning many smaller behaviors. Young children whose parents grew up in Texas and talk with Texas accents usually say their first words with the same accents as their parents. Children whose parents love dogs and keep one in the house usually learn very quickly how to play with dogs and be kind to them. Children whose parents are interested in their home and do many things around the house to keep it looking nice are likely to involve themselves in the same kinds of tasks.

Showing Children How to Improve Old Behaviors. Observing and imitating models also helps children perfect behaviors they have already begun to learn. Children who eat dinner regularly with their families don't have to guess about the correct way to hold a fork or a spoon. By the time their parents give them a spoon or fork to hold themselves, they already have had opportunities to see just how it should be held. Thus, observation and imitation decrease the length of time it takes children to learn many everyday skills. Trial-and-error learning is avoided.

Many behaviors that children develop in school are also perfected through observation and imitation. In this case, the model usually is the teacher and the behaviors learned are academic skills. Some good examples are the development of reading and writing skills in which teachers demonstrate the correct way to proceed and then give the children the opportunity to imitate.

PRINCIPLE 1: "Do as I say, not as I do" just doesn't work with children. Parents who want their children to behave in certain ways need to act in those ways themselves.

Bad Behavior

Whether they want to or not, unfortunately, many parents teach bad behavior by modeling it for their children. Often they inadvertently teach bad behavior that children would never have thought of in the first place. They also provide vicarious reward for this learning. In addition, they frequently teach children to resume undesirable behaviors they had long since stopped.

Demonstrating New Ways to Be Bad. Eight-year-old Bobby and his mother were together in the check-out line in the supermarket. Bobby pushed the cart and took the groceries out. The cashier punched all the prices into the machine.

"That'll be $38.50," he said, and began putting the groceries in bags.

Mrs. Christopher pulled five coupons out of her purse. "Here, I forgot to give these to you."

"I'm glad you remembered. We're paying double on manufacturer's coupons this week." The cashier smiled and punched some more numbers into the machine.

"That'll be $30.25."

"Mommy," Bobby asked later, "wasn't the coupon on the top of the pile for ice cream?"

"Yes, Bobby, why do you ask?"

"We didn't buy any ice cream."

"Well, we'll probably get some next week."

"But isn't that cheating?"

Mrs. Christopher smiled, "It's not really cheating. We're not hurting anybody. And with grocery prices the way they are, the supermarket is always cheating us."

Bobby was confused, but only for a little while. His mother had just taught him an important lesson: it's OK to cheat. Further, she had taught him that cheating brings rewards. When Bobby watched his mother get away with the cheating and make a financial profit, the probability was greatly increased that he will do the same thing sometime himself.

Providing Vicarious Reward for Being Bad. Bobby has watched his mother being rewarded for cheating and is therefore more likely to cheat himself. Parents often provide their children with a different vicarious reward: knowledge that, by behaving in the ways their parents behave, they will have a great deal more power. The small child who watches her parents arguing and imitates the hostile behavior of the parent who wins the argument probably does so because of the vicarious feeling of strength she gets. The child who plays "house" and decides that the first thing he's going to do is to give everyone a spanking is probably receiving the same kind of vicarious reward.

Another bad behavior that parents often teach their children accidentally is smoking. Because of the known dangers of smoking, most parents today are upset when their children start to smoke. The blame is usually put on the peer group.

One irate father put it this way: "My daughter is fifteen years old. Sally's supposed to be intelligent. She can read the papers and knows what dangers cigarette smoking poses for her. She's had plenty of opportunity to watch her mother and me try to kick the habit without success. How can she be so dumb as to get herself into the same predicament? I don't know what's wrong with this younger generation—they sit around and reward each other for being stupid. I suppose they think it looks 'big' to smoke."

Sally's father may be right in part. Sally probably is rewarded by her friends for smoking. But he should also realize that for fifteen years both he and his wife have served as models for cigarette smoking. Sally knew how to smoke by watching what went on at home long before her friends took it up at school. And, although her parents complain about trying to break the habit, it's clear to Sally today that they want to smoke far more than they want to stop. Regardless of the facts about smoking in the newspapers, Sally, just like other children, has learned from watching what her parents and others do, not what they tell her she should do.

Parental smoking serves as model behavior for youngsters. So does parental drug use. Parents may not make use of illicit drugs of the sort that their children pick up easily at school or on the streets. Still, many parents inadvertently serve as models for drug use simply by demonstrating how easy it is to use a variety of different kinds of drugs at home, including many prescription drugs, like tranquilizers, that kids know make their parents "feel good." The parent who runs for the tranquilizers to calm his nerves after a family battle should realize that he's making it much easier for his own children to rush for whatever their friends are using to produce what they think are the same results. Parents who want to serve as models for a more healthy outlook need to have this outlook themselves.

Showing Children That It's OK to Resume Bad Behaviors—At Least in Some Situations. Most children learn when they're still very young that there are many behaviors that simply will not be permitted. Most children learn before they go to school, for instance, that it isn't OK to bite. It also isn't OK to hit, punch, or hurt other children. These are things children need to learn in order to adjust satisfactorily in social situations.

After children have learned that it's wrong to be aggressive in social situations, however, they often learn that sometimes it's really OK. One way they learn this is by watching their parents act aggressively. The mother of one extremely aggressive child brought her to see me. "I just don't know what to do with her," she said. "I've taught her not to hit and punch, and it seems as if every time I turn around, she's hitting and punching everyone in sight!" This mother spent most of her time screaming and yelling at her daughter to stop this bad behavior. She spanked her regularly, and this seemed to do no good. What was happening was that every time this mother acted in a hostile fashion toward her daughter, the child learned a little bit more how to be hostile toward others. It's no accident that the mother who punishes her children most usually has the most aggressive children on the block!

Parents, of course, aren't the only models of aggressive behavior for their children. Children learn by watching everyone around them. They can learn to be aggressive from hostile peers and teachers. One popular source of models for aggressive behavior that we'll discuss later in this chapter is television programming.

PRINCIPLE 2: Don't behave in ways you don't want to see your children behave.

Stopping Bad Behavior

Once bad behavior is learned, what can parents do about it? For one thing, they can watch their behaviors more closely and do their very best *not* to behave in ways they don't want to see their own children behave. Parents who don't want their children to be aggressive need to find new ways to discipline their children that don't make extensive use of punishment. Parents who don't want their children to cheat need to be very careful not to show them successful ways of cheating.

In addition, parents need to demonstrate proper ways of behaving. One father who had been shopping with his son found to his horror that the five-year-old had stuffed his pockets with candy when no one was looking. Father and son had by this time left the store and had almost reached home.

> **Father:** Billy, why did you take the candy?
> **Billy:** I don't know.
> **Father:** You know it's wrong to steal.
> **Billy:** (Crying) Yes.
> **Father:** Well, don't cry. There's only one thing to do, son. We'll have to go back to the store and return the candy. It's wrong to take something that isn't yours.

The father turned the car around and headed back to the shopping center.

> **Billy:** Daddy, I'm scared the store owner will call the police!
> **Father:** I don't think so, Billy. I think he'll be glad that you are bringing back the candy. But don't be frightened, I'll be glad to come with you. I wouldn't leave you alone!

In this case, the manager of the store was also a good teacher. He took the candy from Billy and told him how glad he was that Billy had decided to bring it back. He also sat down for a few minutes and explained to Billy how much money the store could lose if every five-year-old who came in stole the same amount of candy.

Billy didn't steal from a store again; he learned not only just what his father and the store manager thought of stealing, but what his father did in order to be honest.

WHAT SHOULD PARENTS DO TO BE GOOD MODELS?

Be Close to Your Child

Parents who make good models allow their children to get close to them. They spend as much time as possible with their children, and teach them how similar they are to one another. Children tend to imitate models who are most similar to them; this is one of many reasons that male children find it easiest to model after their fathers and female children after their mothers. But parents who are not around the house very often or who are not close to their children are less likely to teach their children about these similarities than parents who remain close.

Establish Love and Respect

Being close is important to being a good model, but it's not the only requirement. Parents who love and respect their children and who communicate their feelings freely to them tend to have children who feel and act the same way. Children respond this way because their parents' behavior is something they can understand, exhibit, and feel themselves.

When children feel and behave in ways they think their parents would if they were in the same situation, we say the children have learned identification. When children identify with their parents, they learn easily and freely from them.

To understand the significance of establishing love and respect, let's take the case of Alex, a seventh-grader from a single-parent family who has just failed mathematics.

Alex was terrified when he found out his grade. His first thoughts were of what his mother would do. Would she punish him? Would she think he was worthless? Alex was ashamed because he knew he hadn't tried as hard as he could have; he was frightened of the math teacher.

When Alex told his mother the news, she was quite upset and didn't try to hide her feelings. She was unhappy because she understood how Alex was hurting. She was also angry at him because she guessed he hadn't tried as hard as he might have. Alex's mother had other feelings, too, and expressed these as well. She let Alex know how much she loved him, and that she believed that he was capable of doing well. She pointed out her belief that there were many reasons for his failure and that she could help if they explored these fully together. Finally, she let Alex know that she, herself, hadn't always found school work easy, and that she was often afraid of tests.

From their first conversation, Alex learned a number of important things: that the terrible hurt he felt wasn't so very different from what his mother was feeling; that regardless of his grade in math, his mother loved and respected him and didn't think him worthless; and that it probably wouldn't be so terrible to try again, particularly with his mother's support. Equally important, this conversation helped Alex to identify with his mother's point of view and to try out her methods of problem-solving rather than reverting to imitating his failing peers. Mother and son explored these methods in future conversations.

PRINCIPLE 3: To help children learn, spend as much time as possible with them, give them love and respect, and let them know how you feel. Parents who are warm and nurturing provide models with whom children can identify and from whom they can learn easily.

Don't be Afraid to Establish Authority

Parents who want to be good models for their children need to demonstrate by their behavior that they're sure of what they're doing. Fathers who behave one way on one day and another on another day are likely to have difficulty teaching their children which is the best way to behave. Mothers and fathers who disagree with one another as to how to behave need to decide together what stance to take in particular situations. If a mother on one day demonstrates to her child that it's OK to cheat the supermarket and the father on the next day demonstrates that this is a bad behavior that shouldn't be repeated, the child is likely to be confused. Children attempt to change their parents' behavior with the challenge, "Johnny's father does that and lets him do that all the time, too."

Principle 4: Know what you're doing and don't be afraid to defend your position; both parents need to agree on a position to be convincing.

Provide Rewards

Although learning through imitation doesn't require parental reward, parents who do their best to combine reward with modeling are the best teachers of children. The warm, nurturing parent provides love and affection that all children need and is a parent with whom most children can identify. But parents can also provide other types of rewards.

One important reward that helps learning through imitation is vicarious reward. When parents clearly represent authority figures, children may receive vicarious reward from imitating their behavior. In this case, children who imitate their parents receive the vicarious reward of feeling the status their parents hold. A good example is the child playing "house" who immediately directs all the others at their activities. "I'm the Mommy," says little Janey, "and you are the child. Now it's two o'clock and time for your nap. You'll have to go right to bed." Janey obviously perceives her mother as a powerful person who controls the activities of children. By pretending to be her mother, she experiences feelings of this power.

Children may be rewarded vicariously be observing their parents' success at professional or social undertakings, also. Penny is delighted when her mother's picture appears in the newspaper as Director of City Council; she takes the picture to school for "Show and Tell." Arthur is thrilled when his father's book is published and finally appears in the bookstore window where Arthur's friends can see it. In both cases these children are experiencing pride in their parents' accomplishments, and they are probably learning the value of working at gaining professional skills at the same time.

Remove Trial and Error

Finally, parents who make good models for their children help them learn most easily by eliminating as much trial and error in their learning as possible. The more parents are around to show children how to behave, the less likely children are to go off on their own and try out new ways of behaving. This isn't to suggest, of course, that parents should inhibit creativity; it does suggest that parents who are around to show children safe and productive ways of learning are most likely to have children who don't get involved in dangerous or totally undesirable behaviors.

> PRINCIPLE 5: *Reward never hurts! Remember that principles of modeling work most effectively when parents combine them with behavior management principles.*

WHO ARE OUR CHILDREN'S OTHER MODELS? WHAT CAN WE DO ABOUT THEM?

Baby Sitters and Older Siblings

Parents are usually the most important models for children because they usually are most available earliest in their children's lives. However, children learn from everyone and everything they have the opportunity to watch and imitate. This includes other family members, siblings, playmates, teachers, neighbors, and all the characters who enter homes regularly on television and through other forms of mass media. People other than parents who are regularly in the household can exert a great deal of influence on our children. Baby sitters and older siblings play important modeling roles to the extent that they are present and providers of reward. Baby sitters are important models particularly if they spend long periods of time with children. For this reason, it's important to choose baby sitters carefully.

Older siblings can serve as successful models for both bad and good behavior. The young child whose older brother or sister successfully bullies her and gets away with taking away her toys may imitate this behavior and receive the vicarious reward of feeling powerful herself. If there isn't anyone in the house the smaller child can bully, she may elect instead to throw her doll on the floor or stamp on her teddy bear. But older siblings also teach good behaviors. When Alex's older sister won the school spelling bee and was chosen to enter the city competition, Alex told all his friends about it. If Alex's parents as well as his sister are able to demonstrate for him that he, too, can succeed at school tasks, Alex will be likely to do his best to emulate her success.

Peers

Peers rarely serve as important models to small children because small children usually have far less contact with peers than with members of their own households. But as children get older and spend more and more time away from home, peers become increasingly important. Friendship groups become increasingly significant as children go through elementary school.

By the time children reach middle school and high school, they spend large proportions of their time with their peers, and peers increase dramatically in their importance as model figures. Psychologists report that, at this period of children's lives, peers play important functions in providing reward, particularly when parents are less frequently available.[3]

What can parents do to ensure that peers provide models who will increase good and decrease bad behaviors? When children are young, parents can place them in situations where they will have the opportunity to meet other children who are models of appropriate behavior. If the children who play regularly at the local playground seem rough and use foul language, for example, parents can choose another place for their children to play.

Parents of adolescents, however, have far less control over their children's friends, so it's important that they encourage their children while they are still young to select friends who seem to be models of desirable behavior. By the time children reach middle school and high school, parents will have to rely far more on their past teaching than on the present ability to tell their children what to do. Parents who have developed rapport and the ability to identify with their children will have a far easier time communicating at this point than parents who have not developed relationships on the basis of love and respect.

PRINCIPLE 6: Teach children when they're young how they should behave and what are broadly acceptable living styles; the older children get the more they learn from other people.

PRINCIPLE 7: In choosing someone to take care of a young child, consider her attributes as a model as well as the methods she uses to rear children; baby sitters and other members of the household can exert strong influences on children's behavior.

Teachers

Once children reach school age, large portions of their time are spent with teachers. Teachers can serve as important models for good behaviors, and parents can help them become effective at this task.

There are many factors, of course, that affect teachers' abilities to help children learn. Teachers who take the time to get to know their students as individuals, who establish rapport and act as sympathetic companions, who know what it is they want their students to do and demonstrate their own knowledge, and who are careful to reward children for learning are likely to have the greatest impact on student behavior. Conversely, teachers who are disinterested in their students and punitive rather than rewarding tend to have far less success.

Parents can help teachers who want to help children learn by letting their children know that the teacher's view is important. Parents can help by supporting the teacher, by coming to teachers' meetings, by listening carefully to what teachers say, and, most importantly, by communicating clearly to their children their respect for the teacher. Fourteen-year-old Jackie may think his math teacher is an old bag. But if he thinks a lot of his father's judgment and his father lets it be known that he thinks Miss Durkey really knows her math, Jackie will probably be willing to take her more seriously.

TV

Television has brought into our homes a wide variety of new heroes and heroines who teach both good and bad behaviors. American children watch TV an average of six hours a day, mostly unmonitored by parents. Some psychologists have reported that by the time American children reach sixteen, they have spent far more time watching TV than they have attending school.[4] Studies have shown that the amount of time children spend watching TV is directly related to school grades, and that we can expect grades to be lower the more our children sit in front of the set.

One aspect of TV watching that seems to threaten our children's development is the relationship between TV watching and aggression. Many programs on TV teach a variety of new kinds of aggressive responses that children might never have ever thought about before watching the TV program. Everyday, TV characters find new ways to hit, punch, attack, talk back, and destroy property. TV models on some programs seem to vie for new and innovative ways to maim or kill. In some cases, models who commit extremely aggressive and hostile behaviors are punished. However, many who commit aggressive acts not only get away with what they are doing but are rewarded for it. TV programs in which hero-models play the roles of drug addicts or street-fighters provide additional sources of observation and imitation.

Another type of behavior modeled frequently on TV is explicit sexual behavior. TV models find true love and happiness by behaving in ways that can bring observers only deep unhappiness if they imitate what they see.

Is all TV bad for children? Should we put the TV set away in the closet and throw away the key? No, say the experts. It's a bit late in the TV-watching game to take such drastic action. Parents can, however, do many things to control the observational learning that takes place. For one thing, they can cut children's watching time down to reasonable lengths. They can also find out what their children are watching and set rules on what is permissible and what is not. Children whose parents require them to be selective in their TV watching and keep their viewing periods to an hour or so per day tend to exhibit far fewer bad behaviors modeled on many TV programs than children whose parents let them watch anything they want for as long as they want.

A prime danger in TV seems to be that parents often let it take over their caregiving roles. While children are watching TV, they aren't getting into trouble, so parents tend to ignore them. One psychologist referred to the TV set in the American home as a "flickering blue parent" who spends more time baby sitting than anybody else on the American scene.[5] This baby sitter can be the teacher of a vast number of bad behaviors if we let it. Or it can be put on a leash—and used when the timing is appropriate and when the models appearing on its screen are teaching what parents want their children to learn.

In short, TV does provide many useful and educational programs for our children, but parents must do the monitoring. They can expose their children to specific educational programs that teach specific skills, or they can allow them to watch any program that happens to be on. The two choices will produce different learning experiences.

PRINCIPLE 8: Use outside influences on children's development to their best advantage; help teachers by giving them sup-

port; select TV programming that increases desirable and appropriate behavior.

HELP! WHAT DO I DO NOW?

A Case Study Involving Modeling

The following case study (with names changed) came from a psychologist's files:

I. Identification and Sources of Information
Name: Allie Malloy
Sex: Female
Age: Ten years
Sources of information:

1. Interview with Allie
2. Interview with Allie's parents

II. Family History

Allie is the daughter of Margaret Malloy and the adopted daughter of Richard Malloy, the fifty-two-year-old owner of a chain of drugstores in an eastern city. It is the second marriage for both Mr. and Mrs. Malloy; Mr. Malloy has two teenage children by his previous marriage, who live with their mother on the west coast. Mr. Malloy, with Allie's happy agreement, adopted her shortly after his marriage two years ago to her mother. Allie's real father died when she was very small, and she has no recollection of him. Allie's mother is thirty-five years old and works as a receptionist at a firm in their city. Mrs. Malloy has always worked outside the home. When she first married Mr. Malloy, the family moved to a larger apartment in the building where Mr. Malloy had been living. Allie started a new school that year in a new neighborhood. Last summer the Malloys located a large, comfortable house on the outskirts of town in a good neighborhood. They bought the house and moved in September. Allie started her second new school in two years.

III. Case History

Allie has been attending fifth grade in her new school for six months. Although she did well in school for the first three grades, and did fairly well last year after her parents were married, this year she seems to be having a great deal of difficulty keeping up with her classwork. The teacher called Mr. and Mrs. Malloy in for a meeting and suggested that Allie's academic problem was compounded by extreme shyness and an inability to interact on a social basis with the other children.

"Mrs. Malloy," reported the teacher, "when I send the class out to the playground for recess, I can always be sure that there will be groups playing games and enjoying themselves, and a few will be sitting on the sidelines. Allie is always sitting on the sidelines and seems so sad. Whatever is bothering her may be what is causing her school work to suffer."

That night, the Malloys had a family conference at the dinner table.

"Don't you like your new school, Allie?" asked her father.

"Oh, it's OK, but . . . ."

"But what?"

"Oh, I don't know. It's so different from any of the other schools. Last year all the kids lived close by and we played together in the park playground across from school after class. Now it's all different and the kids live far away. I can't get to know them because they don't stay around the school after hours. Their mothers come for them by car and take them off to dancing lessons or gymnastics. And we just don't have anything to talk about."

"Well, do you want to take dancing lessons or gymnastics? It could be arranged," Mrs. Malloy commented.

"Noooooooooo, But I would like to do something with the other kids . . . if only I could get to know them."

"How about inviting them over to the house after school?"

"Now Frank . . . that's alright. But they'd be there alone. I don't get home from work until five o'clock."

"I don't want them here, Mom. I just don't know what I want."

Allie asked to be excused, and went to her room to watch TV.

When the next report card came out, Allie's marks were still low, and the teacher had commented on the back of the card that Allie still seemed to have trouble communicating with her peers. The family decided to seek counseling.

Dr. Christopher met twice a week with Allie for a month before he called everyone in for a family conference. "You know," he told the Malloys, "family therapy is becoming more and more a way of dealing with many problems of individuals who are trying to live together as a group and still develop their own identities. Allie has been telling me how glad she was that you two are married and that she has a family now with both a mother and a father just like most of the other children in her class."

"I love Allie as if she had been born to me, and I certainly hope she knows that," responded Mr. Malloy.

"Oh Daddy, I know that. And I love you too," responded the little girl.

"What do you think is the problem, Dr. Christopher?"

"I'll let Allie tell you what she told me," answered the doctor.

"Well, I didn't understand it myself," answered Allie, "until I began my talks with Dr. Christopher. I was glad when we decided to buy the new house, and I have my own room now all decorated just the way I like it. But I don't know how to do the things that the other kids who live out here do. And I feel alone, except for when you and Daddy are home at night. I am ashamed about my bad grades. I think I daydream in class instead of listening."

The Malloys discussed with Allie and Dr. Christopher just what they might do to help. Dr. Christopher pointed out that the school that Allie attends has many extracurricular activities, and that most of these are directed by mothers. In addition, the neighborhood has a series of organized clubs that, in turn, offer lessons in arts and social skills—and parties. Allie might like to join, he pointed out, but she needs some social support from her family to do so.

"What kind of social support?" asked Mrs. Malloy.

"Oh, perhaps to be a parent supervisor. That would show the others that Allie has a family just like they do."

Mrs. Malloy paused. "You know, I've always worked since Allie was a tiny baby and I was widowed. I was never much for ladies clubs before then, and I'm afraid that I would really be a mess at something like that . . . and make Allie ashamed of me."

Allie smiles.

"Isn't that what you thought she'd say?" asked Dr. Christopher.

"Yes, Mommy, I don't want you to be uncomfortable and I know you're tired after a day of working . . . ."

"Oh, Allie, it isn't that. What if the other parents didn't like the way I organized a club? Or what if the kids didn't like it? Would you think I was doing you a favor then?"

Dr. Christopher pointed out then that Allie's shyness and insecurity probably were behaviors that Allie learned from her mother.

"But Mommy always could do *anything!*" Allie exclaimed. "She took care of me when we were all alone and she never was afraid!"

"Oh, Allie, of course I was afraid. I did my best for the two of us. I worked hard, and kept up a home. But I always worried that people were looking at us and saying I wasn't doing a good job." She added, "I suppose Dr. Christopher's right. I did lots of things that let you know I was afraid . . . like being too scared of the other mothers to help out with school clubs."

Allie laughed.

Dr. Christopher explained to Allie and her mother how well both had succeeded at adjusting, first to the life they had together and then to their new life as part of a larger family unit with Mr. Malloy. "Perhaps there's still one change you'll have to deal with," he said, "that is, if Allie is going to get help learning to feel comfortable with peers." He suggested continued thereapy for Allie and her mother.

IV. Present Status, Diagnosis, and Prognosis

Mrs. Malloy and her daughter attended therapy sessions separately with Dr. Christopher for a number of months. In September, Mrs.

Malloy, after a conference with her husband, requested a leave of absence from her job. She wanted to have full time, at least for six months, to engage in a variety of extracurricular activities with her daughter. Family finances allowed her to take her leave comfortably and her employer promised her her job back.

Mrs. Malloy, with Dr. Christopher's help, became active that year in the PTA; she became a lunchroom monitor and parent coordinator of a number of after-school activities. She became a Girl Scout leader and arranged to hold meetings regularly at the Malloy house. She became active in community affairs and began to meet socially with her neighbors. When her leave was up, Mrs. Malloy returned to her job, but she arranged, together with her husband, to keep up evenings with many of the activities that were started.

Dr. Christopher reports that the prognosis for Allie is good. Now she has two models in her household who teach her daily how to interact more comfortably with others. It wasn't a bad lesson to watch her mother overcome her own fears in taking on these new social roles. Allie had the additional lesson of empathizing with her mother's discomfort and receiving vicarious reward as her mother overcame each hurdle. "Mrs. Malloy was a successful businesswoman and mother before the therapy began," Dr. Christopher pointed out, "but the lessons she was teaching were far removed from Allie's day-to-day life. With her new role as socially active woman, she is in a far better position to teach Allie how to overcome the discomforts of changing environments so often. Now that Allie is more comfortable in school and with peers, the probability is far, far greater that her grades will improve. In fact, her teacher said to expect a good report card next time around."

CHAPTER 3

Children Learn What Is and What Is Not Worthwhile and Act Accordingly

CHILDREN LEARN TO BE GOOD WHEN IT'S WORTHWHILE TO THEM!

If Alice's mother always gives her what she wants whenever she says "please," most likely she will say "please" more and more often as time goes by. If Sammy washes the dishes after supper, and his mother comes in, gives him a big kiss, and says, "thank you!", all other things being equal, Sammy probably will volunteer for dishwashing duty the next time. If, on the other hand, Alice's mother ignores her when she says, "please," or Sammy's mother fails to note that he has done the dishes, both these children will be far less likely to do these nice things tomorrow.

How to Make it Worthwhile: Find Out What Children Want

As the above examples indicate, what children do is affected by what they get out of it. If your child's behavior gets him what he wants, he probably will decide that it's worthwhile to keep on acting that way; if it doesn't get him what he wants, he'll probably start trying out other ways of acting to reach his goal. If you want your child to behave in a certain way, therefore, the best way to begin is to find out what he wants.

Deciding on the best way to discipline would be easy if children all wanted the same thing. All we would have to do then would be to make a list of the rewards that children want and use them at the proper times. Unfortunately, this is not the case and discipline is not this easy. Different children want different things, depending on their interests, personal needs, past experiences, and so on. There are some things, however, that most children want.

Love, Warmth, and Attention. All children I have ever known have wanted love, warmth, and attention from their parents. Most have also wanted social approval. Children who think that they don't get these things feel unloved or unnoticed, and they often spend large amounts of time trying to get their parents to pay attention to them. I call these children "attention-starved."

Many attention-starved children have parents who, in fact, love them. The problem is that the children don't know it. Their parents are too involved with other problems to take the time to show their feelings and interest. One example might be a parent who is so wrapped up in the problems surrounding a divorce that she forgets for the time being that the situation is as frightening for her child as it is for her. Some attention-starved children have parents who have no such problems but who are so tired at the end of a working day that they haven't the energy to pay heed to what is happening in the house.

Attention-starved children often will do just about anything to get their parents just to notice them. For an attention-starved child, any attention—sometimes even a reprimand or spanking—can seem rewarding because it shows the child that at least someone cares. When parents provide attention only in this negative way, they are asking for trouble: they are, inadvertently, helping their child to continue whatever bad behavior resulted in the attention. If their parents realize what's going on, however, they can take steps to provide attention consistently whenever their children are behaving properly. In this way, they will be able to make good behavior worthwhile.

Knowledge about the World and How to Manipulate It. Most children don't need or want attention as badly as the attention-starved child. If your child feels loved and wanted, most probably she wants other things. For many children, learning about the world and how to manipulate it is a very rewarding experience. Take the five-year-old just learning to read who suddenly recognizes words she knows in the newspaper. Her shriek of delight is clear evidence that she is enjoying the learning process and discovering what she can do with it. Another example is the budding fourteen-year-old artist who makes a clay vase in class. The vase takes a perfect form, and when it is fired, the glaze is also perfect—the vase looks just the way he wanted it to. This child has planned an anniversary present for his parents, and he is certain to be delighted at their praise. The most important part of the lesson for him, however, is that he has learned how to make a clay object in just the form he wants. He has controlled the process itself. The creation of the vase provides its own reward.

Good Grades. School children usually want good grades, because good grades are associated with parental approval. (One exception is children whose parents don't care what they do in school and pay no attention to what comes home on the report card, whether it's good or bad.) The parent who gets all excited when his son comes home with a good grade on a homework assignment and lets him know how he feels will go far toward keeping his son interested in his studies. Conversely, the parent who is too busy to notice what his son brings home will increase the chances that this child will be too busy with other things to do his homework.

Material Rewards. Most children also want material things—an ice cream cone, perhaps, or a new toy they saw advertised on TV.

It's very important for parents who want to be good disciplinarians to make sure their children are behaving properly when they are given things they want. Just as with other types of rewards, the child who gets a material reward is likely to continue to behave the way that she thinks helped her to get it in the first place.

IS GIVING A REWARD THE SAME AS BRIBING?

Some parents worry that giving rewards for good behavior—especially material rewards—is really the same thing as giving bribes.

"I don't want my son practicing the piano just because I bribe him," one parent explained. "I want him to feel satisfaction in what he's doing and to get enjoyment from the playing itself. I don't want him to practice just so I will get him the new baseball glove he wants!"

The same concern was voiced by another parent: "Lynn ought to clean her bedroom because a neat, clean room is a nice place to sleep in, not so that I will let her watch TV!"

One point that all these parents seem to be missing is that in many situations, if they don't supply these rewards, their children simply aren't going to learn. This is particularly true when the skill requires some activity that isn't really fun—at least not for a child. Some school work may be interesting and fun. But not all of it is exciting all of the time. A reward—such as a good grade for the day's assignment together with a parent's approval—can go a long way in keeping up study habits.

In a similar vein, very few children enjoy practicing scales on the piano. They may enjoy playing a beautiful piece of music. But acquiring the skill to play this music requires a great deal of time and practice. A lot of learning must take place before the virtuoso can be rewarded by the thrill of audience applause or by the sound of his own beautiful music. The solution is to provide some other reward to maintain the practicing until the creation of the skill is sufficient to reward by itself.

Finally, very few school children think that neat, clean bedrooms are really nice places to sleep, even if parents think so. Any parent who tries to use the enjoyment of living in a neat environment as an end in itself is wasting time! It is far more effective to use another reward, whatever it is you choose to call it!

Weaning Your Child to the Outside World. One important thing for parents to remember is that many rewards are not only important in the beginning; they are also useful *only* in those early stages of learning. Children may begin to learn to read, write, and solve arithmetic problems primarily because their parents are rewarding them—with presents, social approval, or love—for doing so. What we want, however, is that our children gradually develop the habit of learning so well that learning itself begins to serve as a reward. We will not always be there as our children grow up to reward them for what they are doing. In the outside world in which they will live as adults, often the only reward for doing something will come from themselves. For this to happen, it is important that we help them learn the right habits as early as possible.

> *PRINCIPLE 1: Use the reward that is most effective in getting your child to begin doing what you want. When learning itself becomes fun later on, this will be reward enough.*

IT'S IMPORTANT TO TIE THE REWARD TO THE BEHAVIOR

Children learn most easily, of course, when they can tie what they are doing to the results. The more immediately a reward follows a behavior, the greater its effect. This is particularly true with young children. A child whose parent looks at her homework right after she finishes it and tells her how good it is will be far more likely to do her homework the same way the next time than a child whose parent doesn't get around to looking at it for a few days. In the same vein, the teacher who grades a quiz and returns it immediately will have a far greater effect on student study habits than a teacher who gives back the graded quizzes a week or two later.

What's Wrong with Paying for a Good Report Card?

Some parents use money to try to get their children to study harder. Such a parent might say to a second grader, "I'll give you a dollar for every 'A' you bring home on your report card."

Many children feel very rewarded by gifts of money. However, many parents I know believe that using money to reward children for good behavior will teach an inappropriate value system. These parents feel that giving money is really bribing. But whether parents agree or not that money (rather than something else) is OK to use as a reward, giving a second grader a dollar for a good report card is still likely to result in a failure to increase studying. Why?

The main reason is that the reward comes too far in the future to have any effect on the day-to-day studying that a student must do to get good grades. Report cards are not tied, especially in the minds of young students, to the specific daily studying that we know helped get good grades. Parents who want to increase their young children's daily studying need to reward them immediately after they study, not at the end of the six-week report period or at the end of the semester.

Furthermore, grades are rewards given by the teacher for what the teacher thinks the children are doing in school. Often students study a lot, only to receive a grade lower than "A." This can happen because they don't have the ability or appropriate background to do "A" work, or because they don't use proper study methods, or because the teacher, for some reason, does not use objective grading procedures.

Parents who want to teach their children to study, therefore, no matter how they feel about the use of money as a reward, need to do far more than offer five dollars for every "A." They need to watch their children's behavior very carefully, be satisfied that they are doing the best they can with the best strategies possible, and then make sure that what they are doing leads to something worthwhile—right away.

For young children, one good way is to set up a system that provides a daily reward for effort. For preschoolers, kindergartners, and even first-graders, a gold star on the nose can go a long way toward promoting good study habits.

For older children, putting stars on the nose is not effective and might even be perceived as punitive. A daily reward, however, can still be important. One solution that many parents have used successfully is a check list posted on the bedroom or kitchen door. A check mark for every day of demonstrated work effort provides concrete evidence that parents have noticed and approved of what their children are doing. Another reward can be given at the end of the week if an appropriate number of check marks have been made. This method can work well with children in elementary or middle school.

The exact timing of rewards can be critical. It's important to see just what a child is doing when the reward is given. Sometimes parents end up rewarding behavior they didn't even notice was taking place. After Rina, a third-grader, put away her clothes, she called her mother to take a look at her neat room. But her mother was talking on the telephone and didn't look up. Rina turned on the TV in the living room. An hour later, while Rina was still watching TV, her mother checked her room. She quickly called into the living room, "Rina, you're a very good girl—and growing up fast!"

Rina's mother was referring to the neat bed and closet, but she didn't say this. Unfortunately, her mother didn't notice that Rina associated the nice words and the approval with the TV program she was watching. If Rina's mother isn't careful, Rina might increase her TV watching instead of cleaning her room!

PRINCIPLE 2: Don't delay your reward. Be sure to let your child know just why he is getting what he wants.

CONSISTENCY IS CRITICAL!

Children learn most easily when their parents are consistent. Alice's parents wanted her to brush her teeth regularly. Each morning, Alice's mother announced before breakfast, "It's teeth-brushing checkup time." When Alice could show her mother that she had done a good job, her mother always responded with delight. Alice got a big hug and kiss. Her mother never forgot. In a very short time, Alice developed a strong habit of brushing that she will probably never forget.

Busy parents who, unlike Alice's mother, provide rewards on one day and forget the next are often surprised when their children don't behave as they expect. The problem here isn't that children aren't learning but that they're learning something other than what their parents think they are.

Bobby Jones's parents wanted to teach him to brush his teeth every day, so Mr. Jones decided that he would give Bobby ten cents on every day that he demonstrated that he had brushed his teeth by bringing in his wet toothbrush and showing off his smile. One day Mr. Jones forgot to get change, and when Bobby came in for his dime his father said, "Oh, son, I'm sorry, I forgot. Remind me tonight, will you?"

The next day Bobby tried again, and again his father forgot. "Oh, boy! You're really accumulating a lot! I'll have thirty cents for you tomorrow if you're good!"

But when the next day came, Bobby didn't brush his teeth at all. He had learned that he would be rewarded only sometimes. And sometimes was not worth all that trying.

PRINCIPLE 3: Pay attention and be consistent.

TEACH WHAT YOUR CHILD CAN UNDERSTAND

Parents need to be very careful that what they are trying to teach is simple enough that their children can understand and do what's demanded. It also helps if they know why. For this reason, parents need to be aware of their children's developmental level—what controls their ability to do and understand things. There are some things that you simply won't be able to teach your child until she's older or until she has had the opportunity to learn a lot more than she already knows.

One example of something that is difficult for children to learn to deal with when they are young and that they only gradually develop the ability to understand and enjoy is a reward that's delayed. I have already mentioned that a parent who tries to reward a second-grader for studying by giving him a reward for a good report card probably won't succeed. It isn't until children are in at

least the fourth grade that they're old enough to be able to understand the concept of time in the adult way: in terms of clocks and
calendars, minutes, seconds, days, or time of year.[1]

Parents of fourth-graders or older children have found it very
useful to use charts on bedroom or kitchen walls and to provide
daily check marks for good behaviors. To teach children to study
in order to receive a reward that is delayed, they agree to give
special rewards for accumulated check marks only when a certain
amount of time has passed—a few days in the beginning, later a
week or two weeks, and eventually a month.

To help older children want a reward that is delayed, parents
need to increase the time period between rewards very, very gradually. Some children who will be very happy when they get what
they want every day may balk when they suddenly have to wait a
week. A parent faced with this problem has to backtrack a bit,
maybe by providing smaller rewards semiweekly for a while. But
with patience and careful parental planning, children can gradually
learn to increase the waiting period.

SOME CHILDREN DON'T SEEM TO DO ANYTHING GOOD

Often children don't behave the way we want them to, and there
doesn't even seem to be any good behavior to reward—either immediately or after a delay. One mother reported that her four-year-
old made a terrible scene every time they went to the doctor's office.
She complained, "There doesn't seem to be anything she does that
I can reward her for."

Another parent complained that he wanted to reward his eleven-
year-old for having a clean face and hands at the dinner table.
"But," he said, "how can I if he's always dirty?"

One way to solve this problem is to make sure your child gets
what he wants for trying—a little bit at a time each step of the way.

The mother whose four-year-old made a scene whenever they
entered the doctor's office for a shot learned to do this with very
good results. First, she looked very carefully at everything her

daughter did in the doctor's office. At this point, it was impossible for the child to behave properly; she was too terrified. However, she was able to compose herself somewhat in the waiting room, and even smile at a story her mother told her.

The next time this mother took her daughter to the doctor's, she told her, "I know that you can smile here in the waiting room before we see the doctor. Do you think you can smile once we get into his office? I'll give you this nice shiny quarter if you can. Then we can go get an ice cream cone with it as soon as we're finished."

The little girl tried, and succeeded in a nervous smile for a few minutes before giving in to her fear and screaming. The mother said, "That's OK, Debby, you did what I asked, and smiled in the doctor's office." She pressed the quarter into the little girl's hand. Later they bought ice cream.

The next time mother and daughter went to get a shot, the mother explained, "I'll give you a quarter again for smiling in the doctor's office, but this time, you have to keep smiling when the nurse comes in." The daughter complied, got her quarter, and wailed only as the doctor prepared her arm for the shot.

The process was repeated a half dozen times more. Each time the mother required the child to remain smiling a little bit longer, until finally she succeeded in getting through the entire process without a scream. The process took time and patience, but it worked.

The father who wanted his eleven-year-old to clean his face and hands used the same process. He stopped complaining to his son that he always looked dirty. This eleven-year-old didn't seem to notice that his face was dirty, but he always looked forward to conversation with his father at the dinner table.

One day the boy sat down, dirty as usual.

"Did you notice the baseball scores tonight?" he asked his father.

"Sure," answered his Dad, "and I'll talk with you about it when you wash up."

The boy ran out, wiped his face with a damp washcloth, and came back clean on his nose but dirty everywhere else. Father and son discussed the ball game. The next evening, the same scene repeated itself. This time, however, the father pointed out that he wanted to see a clean face, not just a clean nose. The boy went out a second time before returning for conversation. Each day the father asked more and more of the boy. By the end of the week, he reminded his son to clean not just his face, but his hands and arms up to the elbows. The next week, he told his son that he didn't want to have to ask again. In fact, he didn't have to; his son had learned.

PRINCIPLE 4: Take one step at a time. Reward learning each step of the way as it progresses.

HOW TO GET RID OF BAD BEHAVIOR

Children can think of 1001 ways of doing things that parents don't like. Sometimes it seems as if children think of new bad things to do faster than parents can think of ways to get rid of the old ones! The two- or three-year-old suddenly bites her playmate so hard it breaks the skin; the eight-year-old gets tired of sharing his room with his kid brother and threatens to pulverize him if he crosses an imaginary line in the center of the room; the eleven-year-old suddenly gets a feeling of power by using foul language in front of her parents; the fourteen-year-old starts hitchhiking instead of taking the bus. What can you do about it?

Find Out What Is Making the Bad Behavior Worthwhile!

Parents need to be on the lookout for the rewards their children are getting for being bad. Often parents are accidently providing rewards they don't even notice. Children who are attention-starved, for example, may be doing a variety of things to get our attention, and we are inadvertently rewarding them even when that attention is primarily annoyance.

Often it's easy to figure out just why a particular way of acting seems worthwhile to a child. When this is true, the next step is to stop the reward that's causing the problem.

A good example is the whiny child. Most children who whine do so to get something. If parents are careful to pay no attention until these children stop whining, they will learn quickly that whining isn't worthwhile.

Children who play with their food at the table will probably stop if their parents are careful *not* to bring them what they want until they do. The eleven-year-old girl who suddenly asks her mother to pass "the goddamned butter," will not get a sense of power if her mother doesn't pay her any heed. If she wants the butter badly enough, she'll eventually try using a better choice of words.

PRINCIPLE 5: Stop bad behavior by first finding out what is making it worthwhile and then stopping the reward.

What We Should Do When We Can't Stop the Reward

Finding the cause of the bad behavior can sometimes be easier than getting rid of it. When parents are the source of the reward, as in the examples above, they can take steps to stop it. Sometimes, however, rewards come from other sources. Some behaviors, by themselves, simply are fun to do. Other behaviors are rewarded by peers.

Some Behavior Itself Is Fun. There are many behaviors that are just plain fun and will not be affected if parents ignore them. Take, for example, the two-year-old who bites her playmate. She gets a lot of pleasure out of this activity largely because of the power it gives her in making her playmate cry. She isn't likely to stop biting if her parents ignore it. Chewing bubble gum is another example. Similarly, can you picture a teenager stopping using dope because her parents ignore it? To get rid of these behaviors, parents are going to have to take some other form of action.

We can deal with these problems in a variety of ways. We might, for instance, remove the child from the situation in which he has a chance to be bad. When we do this, however, it's important to find something else that will be worthwhile to do instead. The teenager who is beginning to experiment with drugs might stop if you take her away from situations where it is easy to get drugs, but you need to make sure that there is some payoff for staying away. This can be anything the teenager really wants—except drugs. This approach is more successful with teenagers who are just beginning to experiment than with teenagers who have developed drug habits. Finding something they want more than drugs becomes increasingly difficult with increasing drug use.

Some Behavior Gets Rewarded by Peers. Often it is other children who make bad behaviors seem worthwhile. Drug use and sexual exploration are examples of activities that can develop because of peer pressure and peer approval. The fourteen-year-old who has just begun to hitchhike and seems oblivious to the newspaper accounts of the dangers cares far less about what his parents think than about whether his peers will think he's clever. Unfortunately, in America today, hitchhiking is "in" among adolescents, and peer approval is high.

What can parents do when the rewards for behavior are totally out of their control? There are many ways they can approach the problem. For example, they can physically take their children from the dangerous situation in which they are being rewarded and find other behaviors to reward instead. When a teenager, for example, finds it very easy to buy beer or wine at school from peers, a parent may decide to send him to a school where alcohol will not be so readily available. He must be very sure that the new school will be a place that the child will like to ensure that he won't sneak back to the old group whenever he can. Sending your child off to military school as a punishment for getting drunk probably won't work. But sending him to a school he has always wanted to attend, a school that provides a lot of activities that he enjoys—such as play-acting, or music, or art—and that offers him academic and social rewards to compete with the social reward he got at the old school for drinking beer and wine is far more likely to help keep him away from the alcohol scene. Parents, of course, may not always be able to send their children away to a new school in situations like this. They can, however, find new places for their children to spend their free time. When these places provide socially acceptable rewards, they are likely to provide help.

Parents should never underestimate what they can accomplish by talking to their children in an understanding way, especially when they are older, and explaining the dangers of seriously bad behavior. They can discuss the issues, appealing in a sensitive manner to their children's reasoning. Parents who understand their children and have loving and respectful relationships with them have a far better chance of succeeding than parents who have no such relationship. Parents who practice what they preach and are themselves good models of the behavior they want in their children have the best chances.

Finally, with no parental intervention, the eight-year-old who threatens his kid brother in their shared room will probably continue to threaten him as long as the younger child is frightened. The reward, in this case, is fearful compliance. Parental ignoring will only make things go from bad to worse. In this type of situation, it is better to separate the boys so that the eight-year-old can no longer play bully. Another solution might be to provide more parental supervision.

Sometimes We Can Stop the Reward Only Part of the Time. Even if the reward for bad behavior is coming from a parent and not from other sources, ignoring the behavior will work only if we ignore it 100 percent of the time. Take temper tantrums.

One parent complained that whenever her three-year-old son wanted something like a piece of candy or the chance to stay up a little later, he kicked his feet and banged his head as hard as he could. Later he would collapse into sobbing. The mother decided rightly that the only way to deal with these tantrums was to ignore them.

Every time a tantrum occurred, the mother looked away. If the noise got unbearable, she got up and left the child in the room, kicking and screaming by himself. As the child gradually learned that this behavior wasn't getting any attention, he slowly diminished the number and intensity of the tantrums, although he tried out a full-blown one now and then.

One day, however, the mother took the three-year-old to the bank. While they waited in line at the teller's window, he demanded an ice cream cone.

"Not now, Bobby," responded his mother.

Bobby threw himself on the floor, kicked his feet, banged his head as hard as he could, and screamed loudly. Everyone stopped to watch. His mother picked him up by one arm and dragged him to his feet.

"Stop that behavior this minute," she commanded. Bobby continued to cry. It was then that his mother erred.

"If I get you the ice cream cone," she said, "will you stop so I can finish what I have to do in the bank?"

Bobby grinned, "I want chocolate."

The next afternoon, Bobby and his mother went to the supermarket. Bobby wanted a candy bar. His mother's negative response quickly brought on another tantrum.

Bobby had learned two very important facts. First, even if you don't usually get rewarded for tantrums, you may eventually get what you want. Second, the best time to get what you want by throwing a tantrum is when people are around.

Behavior that is occasionally rewarded can be very difficult to get rid of. Parents who know that they should ignore a temper tantrum must realize at the outset that they must ignore it under *all* conditions.

The only way Bobby's mother was able to teach Bobby to stop having tantrums was to start all over at the beginning. This time she kept Bobby out of public places so long as there was a possibility that he would throw another tantrum.

PRINCIPLE 6: Consistency is as important in getting rid of bad behavior as it is in increasing good behavior. Remember that it's important that bad behavior goes unrewarded 100 percent of the time, not just most of the time.

What We Should Do When Behavior Can't Be Ignored

Some behavior is too dangerous to ignore or can't be ignored for other reasons. We can't ignore the three-year-old who runs out in the street unless we want to run the risk of having her hit by a car. We can't allow a child to bite her playmates.

What can we do? First, of course, we need to stop the behavior immediately. The parent of the three-year-old who runs into the street needs to retrieve her at once. The parent of the biter needs to physically restrain her daughter so that she can't continue to hurt the other child.

In the longer run, there are a number of ways to deal with these problems. Some involve changing the situations so that it's impossible for the children to behave like that again. Other times it is necessary to let children learn the hard way. When nothing else works, punishment is sometimes the only answer.

Change the Situation. One way to get rid of bad behavior is to change the situation so that the child won't be able to keep on behaving that way. We could provide an additional babysitter who is always there to keep the child from running into the street, or we could put her into a fenced-in backyard; we could supervise the biter more closely, or we could put her away from other children until she learned not to bite. Or take another example, of a toddler who, left to her own devices, pulls off her diapers, takes her feces out, and then plays with them, smearing them all over herself and the walls.

I helped one distraught mother deal with this problem. I began by asking her when the baby usually moved her bowels (she was not yet toilet trained).

"It usually happens during her nap," explained the mother.

We developed a plan. The mother left the nursery door open so that she would be able to hear when the child first stirred from her nap. At this point, the mother came in, gently awakened the child, and took her to change her diaper. The little girl never again had the opportunity to be alone for any period of time with a full diaper, and, in this case, the bad behavior never occurred again.

Playing with feces makes a terrible mess, but it is a common, normal behavior among small children with the opportunity to do so. Ordinarily, it has no detrimental effect on psychological development unless it is handled brutally by distraught parents.

Let the Results of Behavior Do the Teaching. Sometimes it's impossible to get rid of a behavior by ignoring it, either because the behavior is self-rewarding or because it's rewarded by people outside the parents' control. Similarly, there are occasions when changing the situation so that the child is no longer in a position to continue behaving that way is not possible. What should we do then? If the behavior is annoying but not dangerous, one way to deal with it is to let it continue and reap its own results.

Sometimes, whether we like it or not, children do some of their best learning the hard way. Remember, it's not always possible to defend children against all situations in which they might not be pleased with the results. Some annoying behaviors are very good ones to use in learning important lessons.

Take the ten-year-old who gets so engrossed in playing that he regularly comes home late for supper. Every evening his mother complains, but she pulls a warmed-over supper out of the oven for him. The boy apologizes, but he does it again the next day. What should these parents do? In this case, mother and father met with the boy and gave him the following warning: "The next time you come in late, we're going to eat supper without you. You'll have to go to bed without anything to eat."

The boy came in late again the following evening. "I'm really sorry—we were so wrapped up in the last inning of the ballgame," he explained, "that I forgot again. I'm sorry."

"I'm sorry, too," said his mother.

"Can't I have anything to eat?" the child asked.

"I'm sorry about that, too, but no," responded the mother. She went about her work cleaning up the kitchen. That was the last time this boy was late for dinner.

Sometimes parents teach children by letting them learn the results of their behavior themselves, even when those results involve people outside the immediate family. For example, sixteen-year-old Alice had been cutting classes frequently. Her parents warned that she'd get into trouble but she continued anyway. One evening she came home and confessed that she had cut classes and forged her father's signature on an absence note. The guidance counselor had detected it.

Alice was afraid that the guidance counselor would call home. "Would you please tell him that I was home with a cold, Dad? I promise never to do it again. I've learned my lesson."

Her Dad answered, "But you weren't home with a cold. I can't lie for you."

"But what'll happen to me, Dad?"

"I don't know. But I'll go down to the counselor's office with you and see what we can do. I'll be glad to help you any way I can, except by lying."

The counselor did telephone, and Alice's father made an appointment to meet with him to discuss Alice's problem. He told the counselor that Alice had forged his signature on the absence slip, but that that was the first time Alice had ever gotten into trouble before. He offered to supervise Alice more carefully at home. The counselor decided that Alice would have two weeks of after-school detentions as a penalty for her cutting. But, because of her father's offer to help, he did not recommend suspension. Alice didn't cut again.

Sometimes parents today need to deal with far more serious delinquent behaviors. Schoolchildren frequently vandalize and commit far more serious crimes. What should parents do when they find out? Obviously, ignoring the unwanted behavior won't help here. It may be impossible to change the situation. The parents, if they are sensitive to their child's needs and communicate easily with him, may be successful in talking him out of what he is doing. When all else fails, however, the parent has to let him learn the hard way— through the consequences of his actions.

Parents who use their influence with the authorities to try to help their children escape punishment when they are caught in delinquent acts will probably only teach them that it's all right to be delinquent—someone will always be there to bail them out. If the teenager who vandalizes the school building is caught by the authorities, the best thing his parents can do is to offer moral support and understanding, and emotional support in dealing with the consequences the child will have to face. The parent who uses bribery to get his child off the hook is likely to face a more serious crime the next time around.

PRINCIPLE 7: Don't be afraid to let your child learn the hard way sometimes.

Use Time-Out

Sometimes when a child is acting badly, both she and her parents are so upset that it's impossible to come up with a rational solution. When this happens, one useful solution is to take a "time-out." One parent wanted her daughter to learn to discuss her school work in a calm, rational way. Instead, the daughter was usually sullen and argumentative and always responded to questions with highly emotional, loud, and dramatic statements. Since she usually began by yelling and ended up hysterical, it was impossible for her parents to reward calm and rational conversation. One day, the girl brought home her report card and began screaming, "That lousy teacher has it in for me. I'm tired of all this shit!"

The mother quietly took the girl by the hand and led her to the other room.

"Now you stay there until you're calmer. When you're ready to talk quietly with me about school, please come back and we'll talk."

The girl wasn't convinced, and for a few minutes yelled loudly from the other room. When she came back, still yelling, her mother once again took her by the hand and returned her to the other room.

"When you talk quietly," she said, "we'll resume our discussion."

This time the girl listened. After about fifteen minutes, she came back and began the discussion. It was clear this time that what she wanted was her mother's help about one of her grades which she thought was unfair. Her mother waited until the daughter discussed the report card in quiet tones and presented her views in a rational way. Then the mother complimented her on her behavior and gave her daughter some advice about how to approach the teacher to find out why her grade was so bad.

"I'll go with you if you want," she offered.

"No, I think I can handle it myself," the girl decided.

Time-out is an extremely useful strategy to employ when everybody is upset. First, it removes both children and parents from the situation in which the bad behavior was taking place. It gives children a chance to calm down and think things over. Finally, it gives parents a chance to rethink their method of handling the problem.

Time-out works well as long as we remember that its purpose is to take everybody from the scene for a little while and not to punish, and as long as everyone can remain calm.

PUNISHMENT

When nothing else gets rid of bad behavior, many parents resort to punishment.

What Is Punishment?

Punishment involves doing something unpleasant in order to get rid of a behavior.

For a variety of reasons, punishment—no matter what type we use—is often the least effective of any of the methods of discipline we've discussed so far. If used carefully, however, it does sometimes help change some children's behavior.

When Does It Work?

Five-year-old Danielle leaves her clothes and toys on the floor and continually refuses to pick them up when asked. Her mother warns her that if she doesn't clean them up she will not let Danielle go outside and play. Danielle ignores her mother, however, and leaves everything on the floor. After lunch, she asks to go outside. Her mother says, "Not today, Danielle. You didn't pick up your things. You'll have to stay inside now and play by yourself. Tomorrow, if you want to go out, you'll have to remember what I said and pick your things up right away." The next day Danielle obeys and is permitted outside.

What has happened in this situation? Danielle's mother has followed a bad behavior (leaving toys and clothes strewn about) with a punishment (being restricted to the house). What did Danielle learn? She learned that she can escape the punishment by learning a new good behavior—cleaning her room.[2] In this case, punishment has worked to get rid of a bad behavior.

When Doesn't It Work?

Punishment doesn't help teach good behavior when children discover that doing something else bad can help them escape. If Danielle, for example, had chosen to leave her things on the floor and then sneak out the door when her mother wasn't watching, the punishment she was supposed to receive would have taught her to escape. She would have learned an even worse behavior, however, than the one her mother was trying to get rid of.

In other words, if you want punishment to get rid of bad behavior and replace it with good behavior, you need to teach just what good behavior is necessary in order to escape the punishment. You also have to be very careful that no other bad behavior will allow the child to escape.

Punishment is much less effective when children are older than when they are small. This is because parents have far less control. The fifteen-year-old whose school work is suffering because she stays on the phone for hours and who refuses to get off when asked might learn to be more considerate if her parents take away all phone privileges until she has agreed to abide by a set of rules. In this case, if the girl wants phone privileges badly enough, punishment might be effective in changing her behavior. On the other hand, this same girl might do a number of other things, for example, use her allowance to get her own phone, stay out late with her friends talking, or have a fight with her parents for being so unfair. None of these behaviors is what her parents want.

The fact that teenagers have so much freedom is another reason why it's hard to use punishment effectively with this age group. Take the teenage hitchhiker whose parents are understandably worried that he might be badly hurt. What would happen if the boy's father tells him that he'll take away his allowance if he ever catches his son hitchhiking again? The boy probably will learn that it's best not to hitchhike in any area where his father might find out about it, but he probably won't be deterred from hitchhiking where he knows his father won't catch him.

When Punishment Is Too Severe or Too Frequent. Sometimes parents assume that punishment isn't working because they didn't punish hard enough or often enough. When this happens, many parents decide unwisely to punish harder the next time. Unless the child learns how to escape the punishment, however, the only thing likely to result is a very unhappy child. The parent who punishes too hard or too often is usually the parent who winds up complaining, "No matter how many times I spank him, he never learns."

When We Punish the Wrong Behavior. Sometimes parents, because they don't understand why their children are behaving in certain ways, may punish them for what they are doing and inadvertently cause more problems. A good example is masturbation, a behavior that occurs among most preschool children as a normal reaction to learning about their bodies. Contrary to some superstitious beliefs, this activity does no harm and is, in fact, part and parcel of normal development.

Parents who punish their children and frighten them with terrible threats may well get their children to stop masturbating. On the other hand, they may teach their children to masturbate secretly. Either way, they may increase their children's fears and make it difficult for them to adjust satisfactorily later on to their sexuality. Children who learn secret masturbation as an escape from punishment often develop the most severe anxiety reactions. Parents need to teach their children that there are times and places in which it is appropriate to explore their bodies. Certainly children need to learn that an elementary school classroom is not an appropriate place to masturbate. But it shouldn't take severe punishment to convince a child to confine exploratory activities to private situations.

Severe punishment is always bad when it raises anxiety to high levels. Take the child who is failing in school and whose teacher punishes him for what she thinks is his lack of effort by ridiculing him regularly in front of the class. The escape response this student decides to use is cutting class. He learns something quickly when he cuts: the anxiety associated with his public humiliation diminishes as soon as he gets away from the school building, and he feels relaxed and comfortable. It's extremely hard to stop a child from cutting class once he starts precisely because cutting brings with it its own reward: diminished anxiety. And this reward is far more immediate than the distant punishment looming on the horizon. Sometimes children can learn to stop cutting classes when they are given a great deal of extra help in school, and when they are rewarded a great deal for their efforts. It's a hard battle, however.

Why Not Spank?

Sometimes parents, in exasperation, resort to spanking. Spanking might be effective in some cases and for some children when an escape response is available and the spanking is not too harsh. Used very sparingly and not too harshly, it probably won't hurt children. Spanking is easier to use with small children than older ones. Parents should remember, however, that the spanking can often be more cathartic for the parent than it is effective as a way to teach. Often parents spank when they arc so upsct or so angry that they don't know what else to do.

"How often do I have to spank you before you learn," wails the frustrated mother.

The answer is always the same. "You'll have to keep on spanking until the child learns good behavior to use as an escape." In some cases and for some children, that time will never come.

PRINCIPLE 8: It's not terrible to punish as a last resort. When you do, do it gently and sparingly. Teach your child carefully what to do so that you don't have to punish again.

HELP! WHAT DO I DO NOW?

A Case Study Involving Discipline

The following case study (with names changed) was taken from a psychologist's files:

I. Identification and Sources of Information

Name: Arnie Richman
Address: York City, USA
Sex: Male
Age: Five years

Sources of information:

1. Interview with Arnie.
2. Interview with Arnie's parents.

II. Family History

Arnie is the older of two children. The younger child was born five months ago. The family resides in an upper-middle-class suburb of York City in a ranch-style house on two acres of land. Mr. Richman, Arnie's father, is the principal of a high school in York City. Mr. Richman is thirty-seven years old. Arnie's mother was an elementary school teacher until she became pregnant with Arnie. Since Arnie's birth, she has stayed at home. Mrs. Richman is thirty years old.

Arnie was born with no complications after a ten-hour labor in York City Hospital. His baby sister also was born with no complications; both children are healthy and have no physical disabilities. Mrs. Richman breastfed Arnie until he was six months old, and is currently breastfeeding her infant daughter.

III. Case History

The Richmans saw no evidence of any behavior problems in the family until about four months ago. When the new baby arrived five months ago, Arnie at first became very withdrawn. He didn't appear hostile toward his sister, but he often sat in a corner sucking his thumb. The Richmans noticed this behavior, but they were relieved that he didn't seem hostile and thought that he gradually would return to normal.

Four months ago, Arnie's father caught Arnie playing in the bathroom with a pack of matches. Arnie was lighting the matches and dropping them into the sink. Mr. Richman grabbed the matches away from Arnie, slapped him on the hand, and told him that he would get a spanking if he ever played with matches again. "I told you how dangerous it is," he admonished his son. "Do you want to get burned?" Arnie mumbled something about being careful to throw the lighted matches in the sink and withdrew to his room. Later Mr. Richman found him there, sucking his thumb.

Within the next two weeks, Mrs. Richman caught her son playing with matches on four separate occasions. The first time she caught him, he was once again in the bathroom with the door open, dropping lighted matches into the sink. Mrs. Richman yelled at her son and sent him to his room. This punishment had little effect. The following day Arnie dropped a lighted match into the garbage pail in the kitchen. The garbage was too damp to catch on fire, but his mother took Arnie aside and gave him a long lecture on what might have happened if he had dropped the match into some dry papers.

Arnie was well behaved for the next week. One day, however, when his father came home from work, he caught Arnie piling up leaves in the backyard near the garage. Arnie had a pack of matches with him. Mr. Richman gave Arnie a hard spanking, took the matches away, and told his son, "If I ever catch you with a pack of matches again, you'll get far worse than you did this time."

The following day Arnie managed to get a pile of leaves on fire. His mother stamped the fire out with her foot. She angrily shook Arnie with all her strength. "What's wrong with you?" she screamed. Arnie whined, "You said we could go get ice cream this afternoon and then we couldn't go. I was just playing." His mother yelled, "What ever am I going to do with you? Why can't you be a big boy and take care of yourself now? I have so much work to do with the new baby. I have no time to get ice cream with you. Are you trying to get me angry? If you are, then you're getting what you want." Arnie got his third spanking for playing with fire.

The next time Arnie started a fire was a week later. This time he set fire to one of his storybooks. He was standing on the other side of the room watching the flames begin to burn the carpet when his mother found him. This time she could not control the fire: flames caught the curtains quickly. Mrs. Richman was able to get herself and the children safely out of the house. Firefighters were able to get the blaze under control quickly, but not before Arnie's bedroom was badly damaged.

Arnie wasn't hurt in the fire. However, he was terribly frightened. He stood next to his mother, holding her hand and sucking his thumb all during the time that the firefighters put out the blaze. Neighbors had telephoned Mr. Richman at work, and he arrived just as the firefighters were finishing up. Mr. Richman was too busy to speak with Arnie, but he went through the house inspecting the damage. The firefighters explained to him what had happened, and Arnie's mother told him that Arnie had been lighting matches again.

After the firefighters left, Mr. Richman said, "Well, I'm too upset to decide what to do about Arnie. But we'll certainly have to do something." Arnie listened quietly and didn't say anything. That night he refused food and went quietly to lie down on the living room couch. It took him a very long time to fall asleep.

Mr. and Mrs. Richman decided to take Arnie to see a child psychologist.

"The problem is that fire is a very dangerous thing to play with," Dr. Williams told Arnie during their first conversation together. "Did you realize how much damage you really could do?"

When Arnie didn't answer the question, Dr. Williams changed the subject. "How are things at home, Arnie? Are you lonesome? Do you want more company? Are you mad at your mother?" Gradually, the little boy began to talk.

"Mommy's so busy with the new baby that when she promises to take us for ice cream now, she changes her mind and we don't go. When she says, 'OK, we'll do that sometime,' she really means 'never.' Nothing's the same anymore," he complained. "But I didn't want to hurt anything—really!"

"Well, you were lucky," explained Dr. Williams. "Only your room got hurt and your mother and father will help you fix that up. But why don't we see if there's anything we can do with you to help make things the way you like them."

"What do you mean?" asked Arnie.

"Well, you say your mommy is too busy to go with you to get ice cream. What is she doing that takes up so much time she can't play with you?"

"She's always taking care of my baby sister—washing her, feeding her, rocking her—there's no time left for anything else!"

"Do you ever help take care of your sister?"

"No, Mommy says I'll bother her."

Dr. Williams had a long talk with Mr. and Mrs. Richman as well as with Arnie. He pointed out to the Richmans that Arnie's dangerous game of making fires was an attention-getting device that came from feelings of being unwanted. "Arnie really had to pick a behavior that was very dangerous to get you to pay attention," Dr. Williams pointed out. "You didn't notice his other calls of distress—his thumb sucking that began when he first started to feel all alone. You've got to try to spend more time with him."

"But how?" asked Mrs. Richman. "It isn't as if I'm ignoring Arnie. There are just so many more things to do every day than there used to be."

"Well, let's examine them, together with what Arnie does every day and with what he can do to help, and maybe we'll come up with a compromise. You know, Arnie could get a lot of attention he really needs if you let him help you with what you're doing. I'll bet he'll really enjoy feeling useful, and you'll be very surprised to see how the extra attention will help his behavior."

At the next session, Arnie met with both his parents and Dr. Williams.

"Let's see if we can think of some things that you could do to help your mother and make more time to play, too. Maybe some activities just might involve your baby sister."

Dr. Williams sat down with Arnie and Mr. and Mrs. Richman, and together the four people made a list of activities that needed to be done every day and that Arnie could help do:

1. Help his mother pick up all his toys.
2. Carry dishes to the sink after meals while his father washes them.
3. Clean up—wash face, brush teeth, and comb hair.

At first, no one could think of activities that Arnie could do that would help his mother and allow him at the same time to help take care of the baby. But Arnie suddenly thought of how he could help the baby outside. Then Mrs. Richman thought of how he could help by holding the food and feeding the baby while she held the infant on her lap. They added the following tasks:

4. Help mother push baby carriage for walk in the fresh air.
5. Feed the baby.

Next Arnie and Dr. Williams made up a list of favorite things that Arnie liked to do:

1. Go to the ice cream store and buy ice cream.
2. Play checkers.
3. Read stories.
4. Listen to records.

Dr. Williams made up a big chart. Because Arnie didn't know how to read, he put pictures describing each of the help activities on the left-hand side of the chart. Mr. and Mrs. Richman agreed that every time Arnie performed one of the activities listed, one of them would put a gold star next to the picture of the task. Then, when Arnie wanted to do one of his favorite things—such as getting ice cream or getting a chance to play checkers, he could do it if (1) he had accumulated at least two stars under other helping activities; and (2) his mother was free to play with him. If Mrs. Richman could not play right away, she agreed to do so just as soon as she could. She agreed also to set a specific time and always keep her promise. Mr. Richman decided to set a special play time with Arnie every night as soon as he was home from work.

Dr. Williams pointed out that at least one of the helping activities could be done by Arnie at the same time that he was enjoying a favorite thing to do. On nice days, he could push the baby carriage when he and his mother walked to the ice cream store.

Dr. Williams listed one more activity on the bottom of the chart under the others. On this one he drew a big X. It was a picture of a child playing with matches. "Now Arnie," he said. "There is just one thing. If you want attention from your mother, you must perform the activities that will help. If you perform this activity (and he pointed to the matches), then you will not be able to do any of the things you want. You don't want to get any marks by this picture!"

IV. Present Status, Diagnosis, and Prognosis

The program worked effectively after only a few days. In the beginning, Arnie sometimes forgot that he needed to accumulate a couple of gold stars for that day if he were to be allowed his favorite thing to do. In fact, he enjoyed the helping activities so much that he often forgot he wanted to do something else. When he remembered, all he needed to do was to look at the chart and decide whether it was time to ask for a reward. After two months, there was no instance of any activity related either to fire or matches. Arnie gradually stopped sucking his thumb. Dr. Williams has concluded that there is very little likelihood that Arnie will play with fire again.

CHAPTER 4

Love, Warmth, and Affection Make Learning Easier—and Fun, Too

By this point, it should be clear that there are many different effective approaches to discipline. Parents can help their children learn by being good models themselves. They can also help them learn by being sure to reward good behavior.

It's important to remember that no one approach works in a vacuum, and that each is more or less effective depending on the particular children doing the learning and the parents doing the teaching. All children have very basic needs that affect the ways they solve problems, make decisions, and choose goals. Understanding these needs is critical to deciding what approach to discipline will be most effective. Parents can have a major impact on their children's motivations, aspirations, and feelings of competence and self-esteem. But this impact will be productive only if they understand their children's needs.

MAKING CHILDREN WANT TO LEARN IS THE FIRST STEP

Some children don't seem to be affected by discipline, no matter how many rewards parents provide or how good they are as models of appropriate behavior.

"Mikey just doesn't seem to want to learn how to be good," complained an irate mother. "No matter what I try with him, no matter how carefully I use the methods you've laid out, Mikey always seems to do just the opposite of what I want. What's wrong with him?"

This mother explained that she loved her son very much and that she wanted to do her best to be a good mother. Still, four-year-old Mikey whined and cried continually, employed a variety of annoying attention-getting devices, and generally was very difficult around the house.

Mikey's mother had been divorced four months ago and had just taken a full-time job two months earlier. She had arranged to leave Mikey with her mother during working hours.

"He's really proving to be a handful, and I don't know if I can leave my mother with such a burden. She loves Mikey, but she's not young anymore," she complained. "Mikey is awful to her as well as to me. I just don't understand. He always used to love to visit his grandmother. Now he acts as if he hates us all! And he doesn't want to learn the simplest thing like picking up his toys when it's time to go home."

TO TEACH, WE MUST FIRST UNDERSTAND
OUR CHILDREN'S NEEDS

When children don't seem to want to learn how to behave properly, often it's because they're really interested in something other than the lessons we're trying to teach. Our jobs as parents at this point are first to find out why and second to do something about the situation.

In Mikey's case it was clear that he wasn't interested in learning to pick up his toys—or, in fact, to do anything else people wanted of him. He behaved terribly toward both his mother and grandmother. His grandmother was a warm, affectionate woman who gave Mikey a lot of attention. But it wasn't enough for Mikey. She tried a variety of rewards—candy, new toys, a chance to go to the playground. Mikey seemed impervious to everything other than his mother's presence. The problem was that he became worse when his mother arrived. Even if she came with a new toy or some candy, he whined and cried more than he did the rest of the day.

Mikey felt abandoned. He liked his grandmother, even loved her. But Mikey needed his mother and the knowledge that she loved him. His grandmother couldn't suddenly take her place. When Mikey was whiney, his mother usually was annoyed. Often she lectured him in an angry voice. But at least she paid some attention, something Mikey needed desperately.

All of us have needs we must satisfy if we are to grow and develop in the happiest, most well adjusted way possible. Our early baby needs are relatively simple. We must have food and water when we're hungry or thirsty, blankets to cover us, and a change of diapers when we get wet. We should have soothing and cuddling when we are frightened. As we get older, however, our needs increase in complexity.

Mikey needed his mother. At four years of age, when he was coping with the sudden changes in his life because of his parents' divorce, he became desperate. The problem was that his mother was too busy with her own problems: she had to go to work and nothing Mikey could do could keep her home with him. This was all he could think about. He became obsessed. All his behavior was oriented toward getting her attention.

Eventually, Mikey's mother was able to understand what the problem was. She realized that he didn't need her physical presence so much as her continuing reassurance that she loved him and would always take care of him, even though, at least for now, she had to leave him for part of the time to work.

Mikey's mother changed her behavior. Instead of looking for new presents to bring him, she made plans to satisfy his need for reassurance. She arranged for a time to come home a little early from work, and told Mikey that she wanted to have a special play time with him every day—before dinner. She let him know how much she missed him, and she began telephoning him a couple of times during the day to find out what he was doing and to let him know that she was interested.

Mikey's grandmother also changed her behavior. Previously, she had given him a lot of attention herself but she hadn't ever talked about his mother to him because she didn't want to upset him. Now she began to plan play activities in such a way that they involved regular discussions of her daughter.

One day Mikey and his grandmother planned a cake for dessert and baked it. It was Mikey's mother's birthday, and his grandmother helped him print "Love to Mommy" with frosting on the top. When Mikey's mother came home that night, they had a celebration. Mikey's cake had the place of honor. Gradually Mikey came to understand that although his mother had to be away many hours during the day, she still loved him and was interested in everything he did, not just the bad things. It was at that point that he began to be interested in doing other things his mother and grandmother wanted.

PRINCIPLE 1: *Parents need to make children feel loved and wanted before they will be ready to concentrate on anything else.*

LOVE, WARMTH, AND AFFECTION ARE THE FIRST STEPS TO TEACHING AND LEARNING

The case of Sammy is another example of how an unsatisfied need can affect a child's behavior and how love, warmth, and affection can increase learning.

Sammy, a fourth-grader, had a strong need for parental approval. Nothing he did seemed to get what he wanted, however. His parents were very disapproving when he came home with a bad report card. "Why can't you do well—like your sister Sarah?" his father asked. But his father didn't try to find out just what was wrong, although he exhorted Sammy to "try harder."

The next day Sammy failed a reading test. He had gone over the assignment the evening before, but he hadn't known what some of the words meant and he didn't know where the household dictionary was so he could look them up. Unfortunately for Sammy, the test dealt with the material he didn't understand, and he didn't know where to begin. Sammy began to express his feelings in a variety of ways: he started to show off in class and began to amuse his friends by making noises and fooling around. As a result, Mrs. Morton kept him after school. It was at this point that Sammy's mother intervened.

"What's the problem?" she asked as her ten-year-old walked disconsolately in the door.

Sammy: I hate school and Mrs. Morton, Ma.

Mother: I thought you told me you were enjoying Mrs. Morton's class.

Sammy: Well, nothing I seem to do in that class is right anymore. I guess I can never be as smart as Sarah. And I have another test tomorrow and I don't know anything and Dad's just going to yell at me all over again!

Mother: You think that Sarah is doing very well and you're not because you're not as smart as Sarah.

Sammy: Yeah, I feel like a dumbbell compared to her. I really hate it when Dad reminds me about it all the time. And now I'm going to prove it by failing.

Mother: Dad really upsets you when he tells you that you're not as good as Sarah.

Sammy: That's right.

Mother: Well, before you give up, why don't we sit down together and see what we can do? You know, Sarah has needed help a lot of times, and whenever she has, this has worked with her.

Sammy: You mean Sarah has gotten into this kind of trouble?

Mother: Oh, yes. But we were always able to work it out once we sat down and found out where the learning problem was. Why don't you and I try?

Sammy: OK.

Mother: Well, the real issue is reading, isn't it? That's funny. You know, you always got better grades than I did in reading when I was in school. But maybe I can help you anyway.

Sammy laughed. Sammy's mother went carefully over the reading assignment with Sammy. Together they went to the kitchen and got down the big dictionary. They decided to keep it in the living room so it would be available to Sammy when he needed it. Sammy's mother showed him how to look up words in the big dictionary. And the next day she went to the bookstore and bought a small junior dictionary that Sammy could keep for himself in his room. Now Sammy knew just what he needed to do in order to get the grades that he wanted to bring home.

Sammy stopped acting out in class because now he was motivated to do well. That is, not only did he *want* to do well, but he knew just what he needed to do to get what he wanted. And once he learned that he wasn't the only person ever to have problems along the way, he became confident enough to try. According to Sammy's next report card, he did just the right thing.

Often we think that children don't learn how to behave properly because they aren't motivated. Sammy's experience points out, however, that children sometimes aren't motivated because they haven't learned what they need to do and because they aren't confident enough to try. Our goal as parents is to help our children at this task.

The message here is simple: it is impossible to motivate children to learn complicated tasks or to reach goals that are difficult for them unless they know that they are loved. Parents need to provide love, warmth, and affection before children will develop the assurance to take on new problems and to try out new things. Psychologist Abraham Maslow developed a model to illustrate his theory that we need to satisfy children's needs in a very specific order—from the most basic to the most complex. Maslow hypothesized that if we don't satisfy children's basic needs, they will never be able even to try to satisfy more complex ones.[1] In Maslow's model, shown in Figure 4.1, children's most basic needs appear at the bottom of a pyramid. As we move to the top, we reach what Maslow termed the "higher" needs. According to Maslow, we can't motivate children to try to learn about and understand the world around them (Maslow's highest need and a task generally required of schoolchildren) until they have been able to satisfy their needs first for love and belonging, then for self-esteem, and finally for the feeling of being capable.

Figure 4.1   Maslow's Hierarchy of Needs*

*Adapted from Maslow, *Motivation and Personality* (New York: Harper & Row, 1954).

How Can We Tell When Children Feel Unloved?

We can tell when children feel unloved by watching their behavior very closely. Children like Mikey, who spend a great deal of their time and energy trying to get our attention, probably feel unloved. The attention-starved child wants to be noticed so badly that she often misbehaves because she feels that even a spanking is better than no attention at all. She might cling and jump on her parents and continually attract attention to herself. It's often very difficult for the child who feels unloved to think of anything other than getting attention. All activities seem to be devoted to satisfying this terribly important need.

Sometimes the child who feels unloved behaves in a very different way: he withdraws or becomes seriously depressed. The withdrawn child has a great deal of difficulty learning how to change his behavior because he's so wrapped up in his own miseries.

The seriously depressed child often resorts to fantasies in his withdrawal from reality. Serious depression can sometimes lead to extremely dangerous behavior, as in the extreme case when a child attempts suicide.

What Can We Do About It?

Curing serious aggression or depression often requires the help of a child psychologist or psychiatrist. Children who exhibit extreme aggression, who seem withdrawn and live in a fantasy world, or who indicate that they are playing with thoughts of suicide need help right away. We won't deal in this book with this behavior since it requires outside help (see Chapter 10). Our aim instead is to help parents show their children their love and to provide a happy, healthy environment that will minimize problems of this sort in the first place.

Don't be afraid to touch. Americans often have some difficulty expressing love and affection to their children. Unlike parents in some other societies, we do not comfortably hug and kiss our children once they are no longer small. We find it particularly difficult to physically demonstrate our love for our male children—who need these demonstrations every bit as much as our females. Physical affection isn't a female-dominated activity in many countries in the world. In Russia, for example, fathers greet their adult sons with bear hugs and sloppy kisses. Boys who are friends show their affection by holding hands or taking each other's arm. It isn't uncommon for male friends who haven't seen each other in a long time to greet one another affectionately with kisses. In many European countries, affection for other people, whether they are males or females, is regularly demonstrated with a hug and a kiss on each cheek. Indeed, America seems to stand alone in its apparent fear of physical demonstrations of affection. Cultural mores, however, don't remove our children's need to understand intellectually and emotionally that they are loved and wanted.

American parents who find it difficult to demonstrate affection with hugs and kisses may show their feelings in other ways. Simple touching can be expressive of many emotions. A pat on the arm or a gentle squeeze to the shoulder can convey many strong feelings important to the psychological well-being of children. A father who doesn't want to give his fifteen-year-old son a kiss can hug him or squeeze him in a manner that demonstrates his feelings. The message won't be missed, particularly by the child who is looking for it.

Be there to provide emotional support. Parental emotional support is important in convincing children that they are capable. Children, because of their small size and their lack of experience in dealing with problems, often feel inadequate; their parents' attention and emotional support lets them know they have someone on their side when they are out trying to solve problems in their world.

PRINCIPLE 2: Make children feel loved by communicating loving feelings, showing physical affection, and being there to provide emotional support. It's important.

TEACHING SELF-ESTEEM

Parents who love their children and let them know it have children who are ready to tackle the other problems of their lives. The child with self-esteem feels that she is a valuable person, of worth to herself, her parents, and other people in the world. She is proud of herself, knows that other people are too, and is delighted at her successes.

The child without self-esteem, on the other hand, feels no such sense of worth. He may feel loved, just as a puppy is loved. But if that love isn't accompanied by knowledge that he is someone special and important, we say that he has low self-esteem. Low self-esteem often occurs when children fail to do what they perceive their parents want.

Why Is Self-Esteem So Important?

Children with low self-esteem often perceive themselves as the cause of everything that goes wrong in their lives. Their feelings often cause them to believe that if they weren't around, any bad things that are happening would go away.

Take Lois, a second-grader whose parents invited her class to her eight-year birthday party. Lois was excited because her father had just bought a tape recorder and offered to tape all the children singing a new song they had learned at school. Lois's friend Sally had laughed. "You'd only spoil the song if you sang, Lois. You can't carry a tune!" Lois's father didn't notice Sally's remark or Lois's look of anguish. He got all the children in front of the microphone. They all sang the song but Lois, who mouthed the words silently. Then Lois's father played the song for them. All the children were delighted. No one noticed Lois's discomfort. She was standing alone thinking quietly to herself, "Yes, the song sounds good. But Sally's right. It's good because I wasn't singing too and didn't wreck it." For Lois, her father's and friends' applause brought only discomfort: she knew the applause was a result of her not singing.

Children with low self-esteem tend to emphasize their failures rather than their successes. Bettye, another child with low self-esteem, is a high school senior with excellent grades who has been admitted to two major universities for undergraduate work but has been rejected at a third. Most students would be delighted to have the acceptances. Not Bettye. She is terribly concerned about her failure to be admitted to the third university. "I know I disappointed my parents. I suppose I'm just not good enough to get in there— even though my mother was."

No matter what children with low self-esteem do, they are unable to feel satisfied that they have accomplished anything of value to their parents.

How Can We Tell When Children Have Esteem Problems?

Psychologist Stanley Coopersmith studied the differences among children with different degrees of self-esteem.[2] He found that children with high self-esteem—that is, those who felt themselves to be valuable human beings—tended to be outgoing in their behavior, creative and inquisitive about things around them, and unafraid. These children were likely to talk at the dinner table, ask questions in class, and be willing to make mistakes. Children with lower self-esteem, on the other hand, tended to be fearful. These children watched over their behaviors very carefully and often were anxious. They were as quiet as possible at home, rarely asked questions in school or raised their hands unless they were sure they had the right answers, and tried their best to make their views match those of their parents and teachers. Children with low self-esteem behaved in ways that showed they felt unloved: they were often aggressive and hostile. Sometimes they withdrew, although every once in a while these children were apt to explode in anger. Not only did they feel unloved; they felt unworthy of love—they felt unlovable!

Looking at these descriptions of behavior, most parents decide they want to increase the self-esteem of their children as much as they can. After all, the creative, outgoing child who doesn't experience much anxiety has the best chance of succeeding at the kinds of tasks he'll have to deal with as he grows up.

There are other differences among children with different degrees of self-esteem also. The child with the highest amount of self-esteem often isn't the easiest child to raise because she has enough confidence to challenge us when she thinks we're wrong, and a low enough level of fear that she's often trying out dangerous things. The child with somewhat lower self-esteem is far less likely to challenge authority and may be easier to have around the house; this child doesn't challenge because he's not sure enough of himself to take a chance on being wrong. For the same reason, he usually takes on our value system (whether or not he really agrees with it). The child with very low self-esteem is the one who is most difficult to raise and who needs the most help: he is sometimes in danger of hurting himself or others in his anger.

How Can We Increase Feelings of Self-Esteem?

Coopersmith discovered that parents of children with high self-esteem differ from other parents in four behavioral respects. The first three of these have been discussed in earlier chapters, but they are important enough to warrant further discussion here.

1. Be consistent in your behavior and attitudes toward your children. That is, follow the rules of behavior management. It's important to set rules, and to provide appropriate feedback for following or not following them. The wishy-washy disciplinarian does not help a child develop high self-esteem. Children need to be secure in what they're doing. For them to feel secure that they're behaving correctly, they need parents to be explicit in their rules and to provide feedback. The parent who is tired after work and yells at his teenage daughter one day for playing music too loud and the next day doesn't seem to mind is not teaching her how loud or when to play her records. All she learns is that on some days it's OK to play them the way she wants and not on other days.

2. Use rewards rather than punishment whenever possible. Parents of children with the highest levels of self-esteem tend to be very affectionate and find it easy to reward their children with love and affection. As I pointed out in Chapter 3, it's OK to use punishment sometimes. But too much punishment creates anxiety, which in turn makes it more difficult to learn and decreases self-confidence. Par-

ents who set clear rules and consistently provide appropriate feedback find that they don't have to use punishment often because
children behave properly when they know what to do.

3. Be as much of a model of self-esteem as you can. That is, show
your children that you aren't afraid to interact with others or to
question what you disagree with. Do try out new things; don't be
afraid to make mistakes.

It's not easy for a parent to be a model of high self-esteem if he
is unsure of himself or if he himself feels unworthy. This was the
problem with which Mrs. Malloy in Chapter 3 was faced. Mrs.
Malloy solved her problems by therapy. Other parents who are in
certain kinds of situations may want to and be able to deal with
their fears and insecurities themselves instead of passing them on
to their children.

4. Get to know your children. The fourth characteristic that distin-
guishes parents of children with high self-esteem is equally important. They take the time to find out about their children—where
they spend their time, who they are with when they're not home,
and what they do when they aren't with them. There are lots of
ways that parents can get this information. They can spend more
time with their children, invite them to bring their friends home,
and get to know their friends and their interests. Particularly when
children are young, it isn't hard to get to know the parents of
children's friends. Parents can invite these people over or talk to
them on the telephone about what the children are doing. Finally,
they can talk to their own children and ask them.

It isn't the amount of time that parents spend with their children
that counts in getting to know children, it's the quality of the time.
Parents who work away from home may be in their children's company for shorter periods of time than parents who stay at home.
They can learn just as much, however, by using their time with them
to best advantage. Parents who spend the evening silently with their
children while the TV set blares its message will learn about TV
programming, not about their children. Parents who spend that time

talking, playing, or studying with their children will not only learn more about them, they will also have an opportunity to enjoy them at the same time.

Self-Esteem Leads to the Needs to Be Capable, to Know, and to Understand

Children with high self-esteem have no difficulty in going on to deal with other needs, such as being capable, knowing, and understanding. Being capable is an extremely important need for children to satisfy during the school years. The child who feels capable in school is one who has learned how to perform the tasks required of him there. If he has trouble doing school work and has no one to teach him what to do, he will feel incapable and may be afraid to try new ways of problem solving. Parents who help their children learn how to solve school-related tasks, and who don't push them too far too fast with tasks they're really not capable of solving, will be most successful at giving their children the confidence they need. These children are the ones who will enjoy learning to know and understand the world around them, and who will have the greatest ease in adjusting to new situations as they grow and develop.

> *PRINCIPLE 3: Be sure to demonstrate your love and your warmth, but be just as sure to be consistent. Children need parents who set rules and follow them.*
>
> *PRINCIPLE 4: Do your best to model behaviors associated with high self-esteem; it will be easier for children to learn them.*
>
> *PRINCIPLE 5: Know and enjoy your children. Knowing, understanding and loving them helps teach them not only to feel self-worth but also to develop skills that will make them feel capable and want to reach higher goals.*

TEACHING SELF-EXPRESSION

Children with high self-esteem usually have no fear of expressing their feelings; children who aren't so sure of themselves often are afraid to let their parents know about their feelings because they're not sure how their parents will respond.

Why Is it Important to Be Able to Express Feelings?

Expressing bad feelings is an important, socially acceptable way to help adjust to problems. Unfortunately, children who keep their fears and anxieties bottled up don't get rid of them—they just hide them. Pent-up fears and emotions are liable to make themselves known in a variety of ways. The child with very low self-esteem is likely to "blow up" occasionally and explode with hostility; the child who doesn't feel unlovable but who is afraid instead that he won't do just what other people want is more likely to exhibit his anxiety in other ways. Youngsters who suddenly begin biting their fingernails to the quick or wetting the bed often are exhibiting symptoms of hidden fears. Another child who probably is not able to talk about his bad feelings and emotions is the child who suddenly begins to experience nightmares. He starts screaming in the middle of the night, and when his parents wake him, he can't remember what his dream was about.

How Can We Help Children Express Their Feelings?

Parents can do a variety of things to encourage their children to express themselves freely. They can, for example, be models with whom their children can empathize. They can be accepting and warm and demonstrate their love. They can communicate their own bad feelings in ways that let their children know it's OK to communicate these feelings themselves.

Be empathic models. Parents need to behave in ways that their children can identify with and understand "Stand-offish" parents who communicate feelings of coldness are not likely to elicit warm feelings from their children. Don't be afraid to express warmth and affection, or to express these feelings in physical ways. Children learn through all of their senses, and they understand the meaning of loving as opposed to angry touches. Finally, don't be afraid to express your own fears and communicate these expressions to your children. Children are capable of understanding their parents' fears and failures, and often are able to understand their own fears through their parents. Being afraid of airplanes doesn't make a bad parent!

Be warm and accepting. Provide all the love and affection you can; remember always to let your children know they are loved and wanted. Knowing that one is loved is the first step toward the development of self-esteem.

Let your children know it's OK to have bad feelings. Parents who want to teach their children not to be afraid to express bad feelings ought to let their children know when they themselves feel bad about something. It goes both ways. They ought, also, to communicate clearly that they understand what their children's feelings are.

One particularly useful method for parents who want to help their children express their feelings was developed as a counseling technique by psychologist Carl Rogers.[3] It involves first listening very attentively to what your child says and then putting his thoughts into your own words so that he can tell you know what he means. Parents who use this method are careful not to tell their children that their fears are groundless or that their feelings are bad; the important thing here is simply to let them know that you understand what they're going through. Later, when children feel comfortable with this knowledge, they will be able to ask for help or advice. Mrs. Morton, the mother of Sammy, the fourth-grader who was having trouble at school, used this method to help Sammy realize that she understood his feelings about school as well as about his sister's success.

Another parent trying to discipline his ten-year-old daughter Gloria began first with rewards. This parent wanted his daughter to practice her piano scales every day. His daughter told him she wanted to learn to play the piano but she wanted to go out with her girlfriends too. Father and daughter made an agreement that the daughter would practice daily right after school and that later, if she did, she could then go out with her girlfriends. They also agreed that if she decided that she didn't want to practice anymore, she would tell her father and they'd stop piano lessons. They signed the agreement, arranged a behavior chart in which the girl kept track herself of all the hours she practiced as well as the times she went out with her friends, and posted it on the door.

This approach succeeded in getting the girl to practice. But, the father noted, it did not get her to like it. He decided to use a new approach. One day Gloria asked her father if she could talk to him.

Father: Of course, Gloria. . . . What is it?
Gloria: It's really hard to talk about, Dad.
Father: Shall we sit down?
Gloria: Dad, I don't like to play the piano. . . . In fact, even though I know I'm getting better at it, I really hate it.
Father: You are really feeling very unhappy about playing the piano.
Gloria: Yes. I hate having to be cooped up inside when all the other kids are out having fun.
Father: You'd rather be with your friends than inside practicing, even right after school.
Gloria: This is really hard to say, but, you know, Dad . . . you always told me you thought I could be a great pianist. . . .
Father: It's hard for you to tell me what you're thinking, isn't it?
Gloria: Yes, well, you always told me that, when you were my age, you always practiced before anything. I don't see how that made you a great pianist! You're a lawyer. In fact, I never see you get near a piano!
Father: You don't know what playing the piano has to do with what you'll do when you grow up. It certainly didn't help me be a pianist!
Gloria: Right. Dad, I don't think I ever really wanted lessons. I really wanted to please you. And I think now that I want to stop.
Father: You've only been practicing for me and not for you, and now it's time to rethink our contract.

Father and daughter pulled out the contract.

Father: Well, it says right here that we agree that if you don't
want to practice, then we stop.
Gloria: Will you be very disappointed?
Father: You're afraid that I'll be disappointed at what you want
to do.
Gloria: Yes.

Father and daughter discussed Gloria's fear at some length. "You
know, Gloria," said her father, "It was your grandmother who
always made me practice, and I guess I hated it as much as you do.
You're right: I say I want you to play. But I don't go near the piano
for months on end myself. I guess it's a matter of 'do as I say, not
as I do', isn't it?"

This father never did accomplish his goal of getting his daughter
to practice. She gave up her lessons. But father and daughter together had learned to develop an honest—and meaningful—relationship in which one was not afraid to tell the other thoughts, even
if they weren't always what the other wanted to hear.

It's Good for Parents to Express Their Feelings Too!

Being able to express bad feelings is as important for parents as it
is for children. Becoming a parent doesn't take away natural feelings—good or bad. Keeping those feelings bottled up is as harmful
for you as it is for your children. In addition, letting children know
how you feel about what they're doing provides feedback necessary
to learning.

The parent who says to her teenaged daughter, "I am very angry
with you because you don't act as if you love me, you pay no
attention to me, and you act as if I'm your slave—here only to do
your dishes and clean up after you," certainly is not going to destroy
her daughter with this information. Sitting back silently, seething
with anger and providing no hint as to what is wrong, is far less
helpful as a teaching device.

PRINCIPLE 6: Help children express all their feelings—both
good and bad. It's better for both parents and children alike to

be able to say what they think so that they don't have to act it out.

HELP! WHAT DO I DO NOW?

A Case Study of a Girl Requiring Love and Understanding

The following case study (with names changed) came from a social worker's file:

I. Identification and Sources of Information

Name: Maria DiServio
Sex: Female
Age: Fifteen years
Sources of information:

1. Interview with Maria
2. Interview with Maria's parents
3. Interview with Maria's school counselor
4. Maria's school records

II. Family History

Maria is the oldest child of Paul and Amelia DiServio. Mr. DiServio came to this country from Puerto Rico fifteen years ago, shortly after he was married. Maria and her five brothers and sisters were all born in this country. Paul DiServio is employed as a salesman in a downtown drugstore; Amelia DiServio works part-time as a waitress in a local café. The family is Catholic, and the DiServio parents are both extremely religious and active in church affairs. They are a low-income family, but they have been lucky enough to have two able-bodied workers in the family most of the time. There has always been food on the table, and occasionally Paul DiServio has been able to send money to his mother, who lives in a village outside San Juan. Maria entered public school at age six and did average work. She continued satisfactorily throughout her school career, even though there were periods of time when she needed to stay at home to help her mother with the younger children.

III. Case History

Maria never failed a course until eighth grade, when she didn't seem to be able to do math at all. Maria's mother came to school to talk with the counselor. They agreed that Maria would repeat the course during the summer. But that summer Amelia DiServio's sixth child, a son, was born, and she needed Maria to stay at home to help her.

Maria repeated eighth-grade math in the ninth grade, and this time she passed. In ninth grade, however, she developed a new interest: boys. Maria began to spend all her time with Antonio Alonzo, a tenth-grader. Antonio and Maria cut classes together during the day and spent all their free time together in the afternoons and evenings. Maria was almost never home now. Maria and Antonio decided they were in love.

Maria failed four courses at the end of the ninth grade, and her counselor told her she'd have to repeat the grade.

That night Maria told her family that she wasn't interested in school anymore, and that she had decided to go out and look for work. Paul DiServio exploded with anger. He screamed, "Is that why you think we came to the United States—so you could quit school and work all your life like your parents? Of course you're going to start working—at what you're supposed to be doing. I want you to get that diploma, do you understand?"

Maria was just as furious.

"What do you know about anything? Why should I stay and do those stupid things that *you* think are important? You never did them. I want to be just like Mama, and I'm going to . . . Antonio and I have decided to get married.

"Married? You are both stupid! What's this all about? What do you fools know about marriage?"

"I know everything I need to know, Papa . . . everything that you and Mama knew when you got married. And I know how to have a baby. Antonio and I are going to have our own baby! I'm pregnant!"

She ran from the room after the announcement and slammed the door. Paul DiServio didn't chase after her; Amelia stood silently with a dish towel in her hand.

Two days later, Mr. and Mrs. DiServio and Maria went to the school to see Maria's counselor. The counselor explained that Maria had a great deal of work to do if she wanted to try to catch up. The family told the counselor about the impending birth—now six months away.

"What will we do?" cried her mother. "This girl won't even talk to us. She and the boy want to go ahead with a marriage. And if we don't let them, they'll go off and live together. What are they wrecking their lives for? If they don't care about our feelings and Maria's life, don't they even care about the new baby's life? What kind of life will he be born into with two parents who can't even finish high school?"

To calm everybody down, the counselor suggested a family discussion in which each person tried to explain just what he or she was feeling. "Later," he explained, "Maria and Antonio will have to make some serious decisions. Right now, we need to allow everyone to explain what they're feeling so we can understand each other. When I say everyone, I mean Maria, too."

The counselor asked Maria what she wanted to say.

> **Maria:** Oh, I don't know. I'm not sure this session is worth anything. My parents already decided I'm worthless.
>
> **Amelia:** Oh, my God, Maria, No!
>
> **Counselor:** Wait, Mrs. DiServio. Let's let each person say what he or she thinks.
>
> **Maria:** I'm pregnant because I want to be and my parents just can't understand. I can't understand why they don't. I'm not doing anything so different from what they did. I know that I was born only six months after they were married.
>
> **Counselor:** You think your parents don't understand that you are really just like them.
>
> **Maria:** Yes, I guess so. Why do they get so angry with me? It doesn't make sense.
>
> **Counselor:** You don't understand why they're so mad.

Maria: This baby will be mine. I won't make Mama take care of it. Antonio will get a job. They think we'll be one of those welfare couples, but I think they're wrong. And besides, it's too late. I'm pregnant.

Counselor: You think your parents don't have faith in what you can do, and in what you know you have to do now.

Amelia: Of course we have faith, but you're so young—how can you think you know everything—

Counselor: Please wait, Mrs. DiServio. Maria?

Maria: I guess that's all I want to say.

Counselor: Mrs. DiServio, do you want to say something?

Amelia: Yes . . . I know Maria is pregnant. But there are so many things to talk about. This don't mean she has to get married. It don't mean she loves Antonio. It don't mean she needs to leave school.

Counselor: You believe that Maria has other options that she won't discuss with you.

Amelia: I believe that Maria has options she won't talk about to her father and me. I think she's doing this because she thinks we don't love her, and I can't understand why she feels that way (she begins to cry).

Counselor: Mr. DiServio.

Paul: Well, I suppose Maria thinks I have been angry with her for the past couple of years. But that smart girl of mine stopped even thinking about school since she got in with that Alonzo kid. What was I to do? I hit her once, and she didn't talk to me for a week. I love her. What do I want her to leave for?

Counselor: You've been angry at Maria because she hasn't been doing what you want, and you haven't known what to do about it?

Paul: Yes, I guess so. But I love her so much. And I guess I love that kid of hers. She doesn't have to prove anything to me by going off and marrying that Alonzo kid. Maybe she wants to. Maybe she doesn't. I don't know if she doesn't talk. We could have another baby in the house if Maria wanted to stay home.

Counselor: You think it would be better if Maria stays at home; you love her very much.

Paul: Yes.

Maria: Oh, Papa, are you sure?

Paul: Of course I'm sure. Your kid would do much better if you finish high school.

Maria: Papa, I don't know what I want.

Counselor: We don't have to decide everything this afternoon. We *do* need to start talking about the issues. Maria, what do you think you want to do?

Maria: I don't know. I need to talk to Antonio. And I need Mama and Papa to talk with him, too. (Maria begins to cry.)

Paul: Why doesn't he come to the house tonight? I promise I won't get mad.

Maria: Would you talk to him like you talk to me here?

Paul: Yes. But we must do our talking soon. We can't keep waiting.

Counselor: Well, it looks as if we've started talking already.

The group made an appointment to resume the session two days later. They continued family therapy for the next several months.

After the first several therapy sessions, Maria and her parents found it easier to talk with one another. Maria and Antonio met with his parents and with their priest and discussed the problem with them as well.

The two teenagers, with the help of their parents and the priest, decided eventually that they wouldn't marry. The couple agreed to continue dating one another, and Antonio agreed to help pay some of Maria's expenses by getting a part-time job. But both Maria and Antonio decided they would wait to see if a marriage would work. And first, they would both do their best to finish school.

IV. Present Status, Diagnosis, and Prognosis

The future at this point is uncertain for Maria, although she has better possibilities ahead of her than many other girls with her problem. She plans to live with her parents and get a part-time job. As soon as she can return to classes, she will. She feels comfortable with the parental support she's receiving, and reported to the counselor that before she got pregnant she never knew that her parents held such strong feelings about her.

"I guess one of the reasons I was glad to get pregnant in the beginning was that I would have somebody who thought I was wonderful. I wish I'd known what they thought before all this happened. But you know, we never really talked before. Talking— when you really say what you think—is awfully hard."

CHAPTER 5

Some Simple Rules to Follow

It should be clear by this point that no one method or approach to discipline works all of the time with all children in all situations. Life is not that simple. We cannot become effective parents and disciplinarians by following a recipe.

Still, we can make life easier for both ourselves and our children by following a number of basic rules. I have derived the following seven rules from principles discussed in earlier chapters for just this purpose.

I. SET RULES CAREFULLY: BE CLEAR

Discipline can't begin until everyone knows what is expected. Rules and regulations can be set by parents or by parents and children together, but they must be clear. Most discipline problems come from not knowing what to expect.

- **Make Rules Specific, Understandable, and Enforceable**

Children can't follow rules that are ambiguous. A good example is telling your eleven-year-old to make himself presentable. To you, this might mean washing his hands and face, combing his hair, and putting on a clean shirt. But what does your direction mean to your child? It might mean changing from his greasy shirt to his old blue-jean shirt.

The best way to teach your child what you want is to be explicit. Tell him to go to the bathroom, to wash his hands and face carefully, and so on. Don't make him guess.

Don't make rules you can't enforce! You might be able to get your ten-year-old to clean her room if you make her allowance contingent on this behavior. But you probably won't have any success using this method with your sixteen-year-old who gets most of her spending money from baby-sitting.

- ## Make Rules Fit the Developmental Level of Your Child

If rules and regulations require more complex problem-solving ability than your child is capable of, he won't be able to do what you ask of him. Telling a two-year-old, for example, not to be jealous of his new sibling and to love her is something he simply won't be able to understand. Telling him that he is allowed to pat the baby when you are there to help, and that he must not hit the baby or poke her in the eye, will be far more effective as a teaching device because it is something he can understand and therefore can do.

- ## Be Consistent

Decide on the rules and stick to them. Children need to know that what's right or wrong today is right or wrong the rest of the week, and that your responses to specific behaviors will be the same no matter when they occur. The child whose parent tolerates a lot of noise when things have gone well at the office but punishes the same behavior when things have gone badly is probably going to have a child who won't know when it's OK to make noise and when it isn't. In a similar vein, the child whose parent tolerates sloppy eating habits when no one is around but who gets very fussy about etiquette when company comes to dinner will no doubt have a child who has sloppy eating habits.

- ## Always Provide Immediate Feedback

Chapter 3 pointed out the importance of providing feedback as soon as your child does something you want. In fact, you should always provide feedback, whatever the rule or regulation and whatever your child's behavior. Let her know right away whether the behavior was what you wanted or not, and what you're going to do about it.

II. REWARD YOUR CHILDREN AS MUCH AND AS OFTEN AS YOU POSSIBLY CAN FOR DOING THINGS YOU APPROVE OF: SAVE PUNISHMENT AS A LAST RESORT

Children love to be rewarded for what they are doing. Lots of reward makes happy children and satisfied parents. It is true that punishment can work in some situations, but using reward gives parents more control of the situation.

- **Make Sure That What You Think Is Rewarding Is Really Something Your Child Wants**

Be selective in your use of reward—whether it is social approval, affection, a privilege such as being allowed to watch TV, or a present. Remember that each child has a unique set of interests, attitudes, and personality characteristics, and that different children will not necessarily want the same things. Phil, who enjoys watching "M.A.S.H.," will feel rewarded if his parents allow him to stay up late to see the program; Mary, on the other hand, who doesn't like TV, is hardly going to feel rewarded by this. Since her favorite activity is reading movie magazines, a far more effective reward for good behavior for her would be a new magazine.

The best way to know whether you are really rewarding your child is to pay lots of attention. This is one reason that disinterested parents don't make good teachers.

- **Take One Step at a Time: Remember, It Often Takes Time and Practice Before What Your Child Learns Becomes Fun in Itself**

In the real world outside the home and when your child grows up, he won't always have you there to reward him. What can you do to make sure that he continues to learn? One way is to teach him gradually how to use his learning in new and exciting ways. Once this happens, learning itself will become rewarding and you will no longer need to find other rewards.

A good example of a situation in which taking one step at a time was extremely important was the case of six-year-old Lenny. When Lenny first began learning to read, he had a terrible time and just hated it. His parents and his teacher helped him by carefully taking him through the learning process one step at a time. In the beginning, they told him how well he was doing when he tried his best. Later, they got very excited with him when he began to sound out letters and words. There was a celebration when he first began to read sentences quickly and easily. In the beginning, Lenny persevered not because he was having fun but because everyone applauded him for his efforts. In a while, however, he was able to do a number of things that were a great deal of fun, such as reading street signs and newspaper headlines.

Parents who show their children all the exciting things they can do with their new skills are likely to have children who won't need to be externally rewarded anymore. Their reward will be their sense of competence and the knowledge that their skill has opened up many new adventures.

- **Never, Never Reward Misbehavior!**

Unfortunately, it's very easy for parents to reward bad behavior occasionally—when they're very busy or when their child misbehaves at a time when it is difficult or embarrassing to be firm. One example is a child who throws a tantrum in a public place or whines or nags continually until he gets what he wants. This is particularly difficult for parents who are very busy with other matters, and are being kept from their business by their children's antics. It's hard for parents in such situations to avoid rewarding a child. Remember: it's harder to get rid of the bad behavior later if you reward it now!

- **Keep Your Child Away from Situations Where It's Easy to Be Bad**

It's much easier to avoid punishment if your child doesn't have the opportunity to learn to be bad in the first place. For this reason, parents need to know what their children are doing, and with whom, so they can steer them away from dangerous situations. If fourteen-year-old Harry is beginning to hang out after school outside a drug-store where many teenagers stand around getting high, a parent who threatens punishment if Harry goes near that store again is only likely to produce hostility. Getting Harry interested in ice skating and arranging for him to take lessons on the other side of town is a far easier way to deal with the problem than trying to get him to see the evils of his ways.

- **Take Time-Out to Calm Down**

Parents can't teach and children can't learn when everyone is angry. Get your child—and yourself—away from the situation when everyone is resorting to screaming and yelling. Calm everyone down, and start again when everyone is in a better frame of mine.

- **When All Else Fails, It's OK to Punish**

Punishment works sometimes, but only under very special conditions. First, it needs to be gentle and infrequent; otherwise children are likely to become too anxious and nervous to learn. Second, children need to be able to learn what to do in order to stop the punishment.

Twelve-year-old Jake has been annoying the next-door neighbors by playing his radio loudly when their child is supposed to be napping. In this case, Jake knows how to be quiet. If he doesn't stop after (1) being asked nicely to keep his radio down during the hours requested by the neighbor, and (2) being told later that he will have his radio taken away for a period of time if he continues this annoying behavior, Jake will probably learn quickly if his parents take away his radio. When it is returned, he will be far more likely to keep it turned down than before.

Never, never punish your child for not learning something that is impossible for her to learn in the first place! Your two-year-old can't learn to go in the potty because she isn't developmentally ready. Not only won't she learn if you punish her for wetting her pants, but she's likely to develop terrible anxieties associated with toilet training.[1]

- **Spank if You Must, But Remember: Spanking Is
Often More Cathartic to the Parents than Effective
with the Children**

Should parents spank?

The same principles apply to spanking as to other forms of punishment. First, spanking won't hurt and might help if it is gentle and
infrequent. It's important to remember here that what is gentle for
one child might not be for another. A slap on the hand of a three-
year-old may be effective in stopping the child from touching the
cookie jar again without asking; a slap on the hand of a teenager,
however, might be humiliating and cause deep resentment.

Second, spanking won't help in any learning situation if children
don't learn how to avoid the spanking in future.

One problem is that parents often spank when they're so upset
that they can't think of anything else to do. In this case, a time-out
period might be far better in achieving the desired result than a
spanking.

When you are really upset and decide to give up and spank, there
is one important message to remember: spanking is often more
cathartic to you than effective with your children.

III. ALWAYS BE A GOOD MODEL

Never forget that your children learn from watching what you do
and that they are watching you all the time. Be a model of good
behavior, not bad.

- **Don't be Afraid to Develop Close Relationships**

Pay loving attention! Parents who are able to develop close emotional relationships with their children and who establish strong
bonds of love and respect are likely to have children who do their
best to emulate what they see.

- **Reward Your Children for Their Good Behavior; Let
Them Know When You Are Rewarded for Yours**

Children learn when they are rewarded for learning; they also learn
when they see you being rewarded.

When parents are good models, their children are rewarded vicariously by seeing their parents being rewarded. As a model for your children, you can help this process by communicating your feelings. Let your children know how you feel about that promotion you just got at the office. They might not realize its importance to you unless you tell them. And let them know just what you did to get the reward.

IV. TAKE TIME TO ENJOY YOUR CHILDREN

Bonds of love and respect increase the probability that children will try to emulate their parents. These bonds don't develop, however, without time, effort, and interest—and without lots of love, warmth, and affection.

• Find Out What Your Children Are Doing

Parents who are at home full-time may find it easiest to find the time to show their children that they are loved and respected. But being home all day doesn't necessarily mean you are using that time in the most constructive way. Working parents who are at home for only a few hours a day but who use that time to good advantage by talking and playing with their children and showing genuine interest in them may create stronger relationships than parents who are at home all day and pay attention to everything but their children.

• Take Time to Play

Playing with children is a good way to enjoy them; it's also a good way to learn about them and teach them.

Games of skill like checkers or chess are helpful in teaching how to think and solve problems. These particular games are played on a one-to-one basis and help develop close relationships between children and their parents. An important rule to follow when your child is just learning to play a competitive game of skill is to allow her a handicap so that she can have a chance to win some of the time. If you let her win all the time, however, she won't learn how to behave in competitive situations.

Playing fantasy games in which children's imaginations allow them to go beyond the limits of immediately perceived events and objects gives parents a chance to learn what children are thinking. Let your children tell you ghost stories or pretend to be monsters if they want. If you can play the game with them, you can find out what they're thinking and what their fears are. You can use this information to help teach them that they are strong enough to deal with those fears.

Encourage role-play. When children play the parts of other people in different situations, they often are acting out experiences they want to understand but are afraid of in real life. In this sense they are "taking apart reality" and scrutinizing the parts closely. Watching children role-play, as when they play house or school, is another way parents can learn what their children are thinking and feeling.

There are, of course, many types of play in which parents can interact with their children. The important thing for parents to remember is to take advantage of the experience to develop a close relationship.

• Let Them Know How Important They Are to You

Children need to feel wanted before they can worry about being worthy human beings; they need self-esteem before they can worry about being capable and productive adults. You can show them that they are loved and respected as worthwhile people by letting them know they are and by teaching them ways to behave that will bring rewards from you and other people as well.

• Don't Be Afraid to Communicate!

Many parents have difficulty communicating their feelings to their children. However, communication is important to discipline for several reasons. First, it's impossible to discipline effectively unless parents communicate to their children just what is expected of them. Second, parents can teach children effectively only if they are able to communicate to them first that they are loved and worthy human beings. Finally, communication increases the ability of parents to be effective models. Children are far more likely to identify with warm, loving parents who express their feelings and emotions freely than with parents who are cold and distant.

• **Communicate Your Feelings Any Way You Can**

Talk to your children, of course, but don't be afraid to touch them either. Loving hugs and kisses communicate just what they're intended to.

• **Let Your Children Know You Understand**

Understanding is particularly important when children are harboring unpleasant feelings about something happening in their lives. Seeing you understand and communicate your feelings in a loving, non-threatening way will go far in helping them deal in satisfactory ways with their own feelings. It isn't terrible for a ten-year-old to think he hates his five-year-old sister. It *is* terrible if he thinks he's a worthless person for feeling the way he does. Only you can help him deal with his feelings by letting him know you understand and by providing emotional support.

V. MAKE YOUR CHILDREN'S ENVIRONMENT WORK FOR YOU AND THEM

Look at your children's environment closely. There are many people interacting with them who can help you in your task of disciplining— *if* you take advantage of what they can do. There are other aspects of environment besides people; you can use many of these to your advantage, too.

• **Choose Baby Sitters and Day Care Centers Carefully!**

Who takes care of your children if you must be away from the house? Particularly if you are the working parent of a young child, baby sitters in your home or teachers in a day care setting will have a great deal of influence on the development of your child.

Psychologists have demonstrated that children whose parents work full-time away from home have as good a chance as others to be happy, well adjusted, and well disciplined, but only if the parents have succeeded in finding substitute care that provides all the factors that lead to happiness, good adjustment, and discipline. Furthermore, parents must be happy and comfortable with the choice they have made.[2]

Baby sitters and day care teachers, just like mothers and fathers, need to know how to teach effectively and be good models for the children they care for. In addition, they need to provide love, understanding, and warmth, just as natural parents do.

Parents selecting baby sitters need to know the sitters well, and to be aware of just how they respond in day-to-day situations with their children. One way to determine whether you have chosen the best baby sitter possible is to watch your child's behavior when she's home with you. Decide whether she is behaving in ways that make it clear that she's not anxious or depressed, hostile or aggressive.

If you send your child to a day care center, visit the place. Look it over carefully. Get to know the day care teachers and find out just what they are doing with your child. Walk in sometimes when you're not expected and see. If you're satisfied, and if your child is satisfied and happy, that child care arrangement is working well.

• Especially When Children are Young, Monitor Interactions with Other Household Members

Everyone in the household who interacts with a child has an effect on his development and what he learns. Children interact not only with parents but with live-in relatives and siblings. If ten-year-old Johnny refuses to eat salad and you let him get away with this behavior, you can expect that four-year-old Betsy will soon be refusing to eat it, too. Johnny is a model for Betsy, and unless you teach him properly, Betsy will soon learn a lot of bad behavior from him.

Other people in the household often can undermine parents' teaching. This can be true even when the other person is a parent. When you tell your fifteen-year-old son that he must be home by midnight and your husband or wife says, "No, that's OK, you can stay out later if you want," you can be sure that your son will learn to go to the other parent whenever you tell him something he doesn't want to hear.

How do you resolve the problem? First you must monitor your child's interactions with other people. If Betsy is learning bad behaviors, watch what she does and find out whom she is watching. In the example given above, the best way to solve Betsy's problem behavior is to begin by changing Johnny's behavior.

The first step in correcting situations in which one parent undermines his or her spouse's teaching is to communicate with your spouse. The two of you need to decide on rules and regulations together. You both need to be consistent in order to establish discipline.

• Help Your Child Learn at School

School learning is important to the development of self-esteem. According to psychologist Erik Erikson, children whose parents and teachers assist them and reward them for learning develop the desire to be industrious; children whose parents provide no help often do poorly and develop feelings of failure.[3]

• Help the Teachers Do Their Jobs

Teachers have many jobs, including teaching academic skills and disciplining. Get to know your children's teachers well; find out just what your children are doing in school and what help you can provide.

Teachers can be effective models of desirable behavior. They will be most effective as models if you let your children know that you support them.

• By All Means, Monitor Television Viewing!

The research on television watching produces mixed directions for parents.[4] Television watching can increase or decrease your ability to discipline as well as your child's ability to achieve in school. Its effect depends on how much time your children spend in front of the set and just what they watch. Study the TV guide, find out when the educational and prosocial programs are on the air, and arrange for these to be available to your children. Don't let your child watch a potpourri of violence; watching violence doesn't teach prosocial behavior. Never, never use the TV as an unmonitored babysitter! In no way can it provide the feedback necessary to teach proper discipline; it can, on the other hand, teach a variety of unwanted behaviors if your child decides to watch programs that use models of this kind of behavior.

Finally, don't let your child spend all day in front of the TV! It isn't good for his eyes, his mind, *or* his behavior.

• When You Can, Monitor Peers

Peers do a lot of teaching. Children can learn good behaviors from their friends as well as bad behaviors. You can monitor what young children learn from peers by choosing their playmates and where they play. Unfortunately, your ability to monitor your children's peers decreases rapidly as they get older and spend more time away from home and your supervision. The mesage here is to teach good ways of behaving when you still have control—the earlier the better.

VI. DON'T BE AFRAID OF YOUR CHILDREN

Children know when they are in control and you're not. It's impossible to discipline unless you are in control and are willing to make this clear.

• Decide What You Are Doing and Stick to Your Position—So Long as You Know You're Right

For discipline to be effective, it must be consistent. If you let your child convince you that you are not sure enough of your position to stick to it, you have lost control.

Sometimes, of course, there are good reasons to change the rules. But you must be *convinced* that they are good reasons. You must *not* allow yourself to be pushed.

• **Let Your Children Learn the Hard Way if They Insist—They Won't Break!**

Sometimes children get themselves into situations that lead to punishment from others. When this happens, be careful not to overprotect! If you intercede too often because you're afraid of your children being hurt, you will pay some serious consequences: you will be teaching your children that rules set by others don't count because you will always be there to bail them out. Children who learn this lesson will have a lot of trouble getting along in the world when you aren't there to do the bailing out.

VII. KNOW WHEN IT'S TIME TO CALL FOR OUTSIDE HELP

Sometimes we feel as if our children's behavior is out of control, even when we follow all the rules. If you have this feeling, it's time to give up and get outside help. A variety of services are available for parents seeking help with serious problems such as deep depression and withdrawal symptoms, extreme hostility, and extreme tension and anxiety, as well as other symptoms of emotional disturbance. A brief introduction to some of these services and where to find them is given in Chapter 10.

PART **III**

SOME SPECIAL
DISCIPLINE CASES

CHAPTER 6

Family Situations That Make It Harder to Discipline: Divorce, Single Parenting, Stepparenting, and Working Mothers

Two conspicuous characteristics of American families in the 1980s that have a major impact on children and on parents' ability to discipline are a rising divorce rate and a steady increase in the number of women in the work force.

The divorce rate in the United States is the highest among western nations; almost half of American marriages today end in divorce or separation.[1] This has led to some specific changes in the American family that affect children directly. First, large numbers of American families today are headed by single parents rather than by a mother and father. Second, there are far more so-called blended families, consisting of remarried mothers and fathers with children from previous marriages, than in the past several decades. Today, about one child in ten lives in a blended family.

The fact that large numbers of mothers are working outside the home because of the increased cost of living and the added expense of maintaining two separate households after divorce also has had direct effects on children. Many mothers—both married and di-

113

vorced—need to seek alternative methods of caring for their children while they work.

This chapter discusses some of the effects of these changes on child behavior and on the ability of parents to discipline. Case studies are included that describe methods of resolving some of the problems that develop—both for children and for parents.

DIVORCE AND CHILDREN

Most divorced parents worry about the possible detrimental effects their divorce will have on their children. Often they are anxious about whether their children will adjust easily to the new family situation, and many have deep feelings of guilt about what they think they've done to their children.

In point of fact, it is not the divorce itself that causes adjustment problems. Children usually are quite resilient and can learn to live in new households. When damage occurs, it is created by poor adjustment on the part of parents to life after divorce and by family strife. Children are vulnerable to their parents' fears and angers. They need to have their parents teach them through their interactions that everything is going to be all right.

For this reason, parents who are able to work out their own emotional problems regarding the divorce, agree amicably on the details, and begin quickly to build new lives for themselves are far better helpers for their children than parents who can't cope with the new situation or who have continuing fights over issues such as alimony, child support, child custody, and visitation rights.

These adjustments can be difficult. Before the divorce, there were many problems to deal with and life often was terribly unhappy. After divorce there are new problems: for most divorced parents today, for example, there are economic difficulties involved in setting up two households. There is loneliness and the new difficulty of learning to behave like a single person. It isn't surprising that parents and children both have adjustment problems. Children, in particular, because of their helplessness to control their life situation, often feel vulnerable and afraid.

Researchers have closely examined the adjustment of large samples of American children for periods up to five years after the divorce of their parents.[2] The results have been startling: at least 25 percent of children still have serious adjustment problems even after five years. Half the children just "muddle through." Only 25 percent seem to have adjusted well.

What caused the problems for the children who have not adjusted well? One possibility is that parents have been so busy working out solutions to their own problems that they have forgotten that the divorce has changed the lives of their children just as much as it has their own.

What can parents do to help? A first step is simply to understand that children are usually afraid of changes over which they have no control, including the new family situations that can result from a divorce. The second step is to recognize the ways that children communicate their fears as well as their adjustment problems and do something about them.

Symptoms of Adjustment Problems and What They Mean

Children who are upset may behave in many different ways. Behavior seems to be related to age at the time of family disruption. All children tend to be frightened by changes they don't understand. In addition, many children feel responsible and guilty.

For the preschooler. Preschoolers tend to be less aware than older children of family conflict when it is occurring. For this reason, they often miss the predivorce family and remember it as happy when, in fact, it wasn't. Some children develop fantasy lives about their old families, and make up stories about their early childhood. Children who do this often become sad and depressed. If the parent with whom they are living is anxious and fearful about her new life, this anxiety can be contagious: the child will become fearful as well.

Preschoolers dealing with their fears after divorce often become excessively dependent. Some may follow their parent around the house and refuse to be left alone in a room. One reason is that they are afraid that the parent is going to leave them. It seems to them a domino effect: these children are thinking, "If Daddy went away when I didn't expect him to, Mommy might do the same thing next."

Many preschoolers develop an excessive need for physical contact. These children climb all over their parents, continually patting and touching them. They'll do the same thing to anyone visiting who will let them.

Many preschoolers also start to have difficulty playing with other children. It's not unusual to see a preschooler start to fight with all his friends after a divorce, or to regress to earlier play that doesn't interest his playmates.

Regression is a common symptom. Children may begin to soil their pants, and some appear to forget that they were toilet trained at all.

Finally, preschool children often blame themselves for their parents' divorce. Their feelings of guilt aren't surprising when we realize that most children of this age have inflated views of their own importance. Since they tend to view the world primarily as it affects them, it follows that often they feel responsible for what doesn't work out the way they want. Unfortunately, at this point, nothing they can do by themselves will change the situation and relieve their guilt.

All these behaviors are symptoms of insecurity. What your child is saying is, "I'm frightened of the new situation and I need some reassurance that you are there to love me and take care of me, and that I'm not going to be left alone."

For the school-aged child. Elementary school children tend to have more understanding of what happened than younger children. Parents are often shocked at the intensity of their anger. The elementary school child often becomes as angry at the parent who stayed home to take care of her as the parent who went away.

"Why is Alice mad at *me* because her father ran off with someone else and never calls?" one upset mother asked. "What am I supposed to do about it? Why doesn't she get angry at her father?"

The answer is that this mother is present to take the brunt of the emotional experience; she has also demonstrated that she is more reliable as a caregiver than the other parent. Her daughter simply feels safe in venting anger toward her.

The anger that children are feeling after a divorce is usually what we called "displaced anger." The child isn't really angry at the parent; she's angry at the situation that caused so many unwanted changes in her life.

Sometimes children sublimate their anger—that is, they substitute outwardly loving and often dependent responses for their feelings of hostility. These children often are terribly afraid that if they show their real feelings, their custodial parent will reject them. Sublimated anger may *seem* more comfortable to live with, but it is usually accompanied by a great deal of anxiety: the child is afraid that she will be "found out" and the parent will retaliate.

Another common symptom of the elementary school child, especially in the first several years, is bedwetting. Bedwetting for the first-grader is a sign of both tension and anxiety, as well as regression. Boys tend to exhibit this symptom more than girls. Punishing a child who starts to wet the bed is not the way to get rid of this behavior—it will usually serve only to increase the tension. Usually children are upset and embarrassed by bedwetting. Parents can help by providing reassurance and by being very careful not to be punitive. They can provide additional assistance by waking up the child at regular intervals during the night to go to the bathroom. Some manufacturers produce devices that wake the child up at the first drop of urine before he wets. All of these approaches, however, are useful only so long as they are accompanied by a great deal of warm and loving contact, reassurance that everything is OK, and, above all, understanding.[3]

Some elementary school children deny the reality of the divorce. It's easier for these children to pretend that the divorce didn't take place than it is to deal with it. Children with feelings like this may pretend to other children that the other parent is "just away." They may make up stories about what they did with their parent on the weekend.

Finally, elementary school children, like younger children, often feel guilty: they are afraid that the broken marriage is their fault.

"Why did Dad go away?" one ten-year-old asked. "Maybe I made him unhappy because I was always making so much noise. Maybe if I had been quieter and had gone to bed on time, he wouldn't have left and Mom wouldn't always be crying. Maybe if I had. . . . "

For the adolescent. Divorce can lead to special problems for adolescents. Unlike younger children, adolescents feel little sense that they are to blame. Instead they sometimes get saddled with the "loyalty dilemma."

An unhappy fifteen-year-old put it this way: "Mom doesn't want me to like Dad and vice versa. She tells me bad stories about him. He tells me different versions. No matter what I do, I'm always stuck in the middle."

Adolescents who have difficulty deciding which way to turn often try to escape the situation entirely by denying its importance to them and turning to the peer group for reward. Divorced parents often notice at this time that their children tend to select as friends other children whose parents are divorced. They do this because they feel these children will understand them.

Close peer relationships may work out well if the peer group has values that parents want to foster. When it doesn't, the result can be trouble. In the next chapter we will discuss some of the difficulties adolescent peer groups can get into and what parents of these adolescents can do to cope.

Sometimes adolescents coping with changes in the family situation have difficulty developing close relationships with either parents or peers. In some cases they project all their bad feelings onto the peers, and think that their peers dislike them. These adolescents may become seriously depressed and withdrawn.

Rules to Follow in Helping Children Deal with Divorce

The basic discipline rules listed in Chapter 5 are useful for all children, whether they are from traditional two-parent families or divorced families. It is important for all children to know what the rules are; parents who are clear in establishing rules of behavior, who reward as much as possible, and who use punishment only when necessary tend to have children who learn most easily. Insecure children, whether their adjustment problems are caused by divorce or by other factors, need stability and clear rules even more than their more secure peers.

Divorced parents need to scrutinize their own roles as models for their children. It's easy, when you're afraid, to teach fear. It's also easy to teach children to be hostile simply by demonstrating hostility.

Children learning to adjust to a new family situation need to know that you understand their fears. For this reason, it's especially important to take time out to be with your children, find out what they're doing both at home and away from home, and let them know how important they are to you. You can make it easier by enlisting the help of other people, such as teachers and peers.

Be sure to communicate your feelings of love and your understanding of what they are going through. Communicate in any way that's easiest for you—verbally, through physical expression of love, or by simply being there when you're needed.

If divorce has made you a single working parent, be sure to provide the best possible alternative environment you can. The last thing that a child wants to feel after divorce is that she is being shunted off somewhere to custodial care and there is really no time for her anymore in the family.

Be alert to when you should stop trying to do everything by yourself and ask for outside help. Preschoolers whose excessive need for attention and symptoms of regression don't go away can often be helped by talking it all out with a child specialist. School-aged children who can't control their anger, who wet the bed, who can't stop practicing denial, or who become extremely depressed may also need outside help before they can adjust. Finally, adolescents, who often have difficulty adjusting even without sudden changes in their family situations, often can profit by therapy designed especially for this age group. Chapter 9 lists specific problems parents should look out for and for which they should seek outside help.

Finally, don't be afraid of your children—and be *very* careful not to overprotect! Children must learn how to live in the outside world and get along with other people. Children who learn after a divorce that they can control their parents by whining, crying, or being sullen are not going to learn how to get along. Children who insist on learning the hard way may sometimes get hurt. Don't try to prevent *all* hurt—that's impossible. But do your best to be there to help when help is needed.

SINGLE PARENTING

One result of the high divorce rate is the growing number of single parents. In 1970 the proportion of children under eighteen living with one parent was 11 percent; by 1980, the proportion had increased to 19 percent, including almost one of every five families with children in the home.[4] Single parenting can occur because of other forms of family disruption as well as divorce. These include desertion, widowhood, out-of-wedlock pregnancy, and the fact that women with children but no husbands are more likely today to remain independent than to live with relatives.

Most single parents today are mothers, although a half-million fathers are now raising their minor children alone. These fathers must make psychological adjustments somewhat different from those of women. Whereas a major problem for single mothers who haven't worked previously outside the home is finding a well-paying job, the new tasks facing most single fathers revolve around child-rearing and household responsibilities.

No matter what the sex of the single parent, parenting without a partner can be extremely stressful. There is the realization that you and you alone are responsible for the care and protection of your child. There are added economic and social pressures with which to cope. Everyone must learn how to make do with less.

Single parents complain that schools have not yet accepted that for many children the "normal" family is a one-parent family. Many schools continue to offer activities such as the annual "Breakfast with Dad" and "Mother's Visiting Day." Courses such as "Family Life," offered in some schools, describe the "normal" family as having a natural mother and father and two or more children: the implication is that other family configurations are abnormal. Single parents are sometimes pitted against parents without custody in gaining access to school records.

Another difficult task for many single parents is balancing the roles of parent and independent adult. The single parent, for example, needs to decide what to do if he or she wants to date or have a satisfactory sex life. These decisions affect children; if they aren't made with both the parent's and the child's adjustment in mind, there are likely to be problems.

Adjustment Problems of Children

Adjustment problems of children learning to live in single-parent families were just described as part of the discussion of divorce. Children who have lived as long as they can remember in a single-parent family don't have the recent disruptive family change that children of a recent divorce have, of course. The most successful single-parent family is most likely to be one in which the parent is happy in his or her situation and provides attentive and loving care. Many single parents, however, are so burdened by their perceived problems that they're unable to provide sufficient attention and understanding. When this happens, the fears and anxieties expressed by many children after divorce occur.

Rules to Follow

The rules suggested for helping children deal with divorce are appropriate for most children of single families: follow the best principles of behavior management, be a good model, take time to communicate your love and understanding, and pay attention to your child's call for help.

Children in single-parent families often need special understanding in dealing with school situations in which they feel different. You may not be able to change the fact that your child's school has a "Breakfast with Dad" or a "Mother's Visiting Day." You can, however, alert your child's teachers to his sensitivity about the special program. And you can talk the problem out with your child, realizing that if he can express his anger to you and you can communicate your understanding, he will be less likely to "act out" in some other way.

Finally, learn to resolve the problems of "role overload" and "role balancing." If you work full-time to balance your budget and there's no way for you to attend your child's school function, don't waste time wallowing in guilt. See if you can arrange for your former spouse to attend, or, if this is not possible, make a special appointment with your child's teacher to learn what she's doing at school. Communication is important here: if your child is upset that you could not attend a school function, be sure she understands that you wanted to attend as well as just why you couldn't.

Other ways of reducing your day-to-day, time-consuming tasks include cooperative efforts with other single parents. Establishing a baby-sitting cooperative in which parents share baby-sitting time with each other instead of paying money allows many parents to spend some relaxed time away from the house when they might not be able to otherwise. Making cooperative arrangements to transport children to and from day care centers provides similar increased free time.

What can you do to balance your roles as parent and independent adult? Can you be a good parent, enjoy your outside work, and have a social life that is satisfactory for you at the same time? You can, but you must be honest with your child. Let him know that it is important for you to play *all* these roles. Be sure to communicate the fact that one role does not preclude the other.

Finally, remember that whatever you decide to do, you are a model for your child. Your relationship with other people is likely to be imitated. It is impossible to say to your child, "do as I say" and not expect her to do as you do. For this reason, many parents of school-aged and adolescent children find it wise to keep their sex lives out of the household.

STEPPARENTING

Although men are somewhat more likely to remarry than women, the remarriage rates after divorce are high for both sexes. Remarriages present new challenges and stresses not encountered in first marriages. Remarried couples often encounter strains from stepparent-stepchildren relationships as well as financial difficulties resulting from obligations to more than one family. One important cause of tension in blended families is ex-spouses who sometimes interfere and cause resentments, particularly in relation to the raising of children.

Children who survive a marital breakup and adjust to living with a single parent often aren't ready to make the next step—adjusting to a new relationship with a stepparent in an entirely new household.

Blended families bring with them a myriad of problems for stepparents as well as children. "For better or worse," complained one stepparent, "when you're raising someone else's children, it's self-conscious parenting. . . . You're damned if you do and damned if you don't."

Stepfathers of adolescent girls sometimes become frightened that their stepchildren do not seem to be aware of appropriate incest taboos. One stepparent reported, for example, "I wasn't really seeking to become a father, certainly not to a beautiful sixteen-year-old girl with two sisters who are sure to be as beautiful as she is when they get a bit older. But I fell in love with my wife, Janey, and there she was with her children. They came along as part of the package— along with their father whom they visit every other weekend. So we were married. It didn't take long before I became afraid that I was holding a package that was ticking and likely to explode."

This father was afraid of his feelings and needed to talk with a professional therapist to work them out.

Types of Adjustment Problems to Expect

Adjusting to a blended family can create a number of problems for insecure children. First, if they are not sure of their parent's love for them, they may be afraid that the stepparent will take it away. Children who still have close contact with their noncustodial parent may feel divided loyalties, and resent the stepparent. Feelings of divided loyalties can be exacerbated by interfering noncustodial parents, who convince their children that the stepparent's directions are no good.

Sometimes girls, still angry with their mothers, take an opposite position and try to compete with their mother for their stepfather's affection. This was the problem of the stepfather described earlier. The final resolution of this problem required a great deal of understanding on the part of husband, wife, and daughter. It also required a great deal of love and compassion.

Sometimes children in blended families find themselves not only with new stepparents but new stepsisters and stepbrothers as well. If they don't learn to accept these other children, deep resentments over competition for love may be the result.

What Stepparents Should Do

The first step in being a good stepparent is to recognize at the outset that you aren't going to be a parent—unless your stepchild is very young and there's no noncustodial parent in his life. Stepparenting, particularly with older children, can be satisfying, but it's different from parenting.

Recognize your stepchild's fears and let him know that you understand them. You aren't taking his mother's or his father's love away; you are providing a new and, hopefully, very close friend.

Try not to punish unwanted behaviors learned from the noncustodial parent. This can lead to feelings of divided loyalties. This doesn't mean you have to accept these behaviors in your own household; you and your new spouse together can teach gently that what is acceptable in one household is not necessarily acceptable in another.

Don't try to compete with the noncustodial parent for love. You will only succeed in increasing tension and anxiety, and build resentments. It's not your stepchild's fault that she has another parent; with a great deal of attention, affection, and understanding, she can develop a strong or stronger relationship with you, and maintain a separate one with her noncustodial parent!

Work at developing relationships. One stepparent pointed out how hard it is to develop relationships similar to those that exist in other families. These relationships take "some getting used to," he commented, "but they can be made."

At first this stepfather tried everything with his new kids—taking them to the zoo on the weekends they stayed home with their mother and him, playing softball with them after work. He felt himself being watched by everyone in his wife's family—under great pressure to succeed, to measure up. But there were no cues to guide him.

"You see, although I was old enough to be a father, I hadn't had any kids of my own in my first marriage, and here were two little boys fresh from a bruising divorce. At first I thought they just hated me. Now I realize that it was more complicated. We have to learn that we have ties through my wife to one another, and build a relationship on that."

Finally, remember that stepparenting usually is a difficult role to learn to play; don't be upset when you have new problems or fail at some of the solutions you try. Seek outside help if you think you aren't able to communicate, but don't give up.

WORKING MOTHERS

Many mothers today—both married and single—enter the full-time work force out of economic necessity. In addition, increasing numbers of mothers of small children work outside the home because they are pursuing careers.

One difficulty facing families of working mothers is the rigidity and unresponsiveness of the work place; it's difficult for parents who must be at work at an early hour themselves to take time to pay attention to their children in the mornings; in the evenings they may be available but are often too tired.

A second difficulty is providing adequate alternative care for children when there is no adult in the home. Chapter 5 stressed the importance of finding baby sitters who will do the same jobs as parents while parents are away. Unfortunately in America today, it is often difficult to find baby sitters or day care facilities that provide surrogate care that meets the real needs of children.

Working mothers often are under stress from the burdensome

task of having to play working and maternal roles simultaneously and not succeeding fully at either. When women having difficulty coping with a divorce have to enter the work force, the problems are magnified. Sometimes these mothers find it difficult to fulfill any of the roles they are required to play.

Types of Adjustment Problems to Expect

Children who are placed with baby sitters or in day care centers providing inadequate care are likely to develop a variety of symptoms. They may become hostile and aggressive; they may develop a series of attention-getting behaviors; they may become withdrawn and depressed. All of these behaviors are indicative of feelings of being unloved and unwanted.

"Latchkey children"—children who come home after school to empty houses—often develop the same symptoms. As they get older, many of these children turn to peers for the love and attention they feel they didn't get at home. If the peer group they select teaches them socially acceptable behaviors, it can be a big help in soci. ation. If not, serious behavior problems can develop.

Children who are still adjusting to family changes caused by divorce and whose mothers then suddenly leave them to go to work may exhibit a variety of symptoms associated with feeling unloved and unwanted. In addition, these children often harbor fears of the future and of their ability to adjust to whatever will come.

What Working Mothers Should Do

What can you, as a working mother, do to help your children adjust?

First, you can reduce "role overload" as much as possible. Many mothers pursuing careers choose to work part-time during their children's preschool years so as to be more available. Some husbands and career wives divide the responsibility by each working half- or three-quarters time. This arrangement often can solve some of the child-rearing problems, such as having a parent at home when a child comes home from school. However, it isn't very useful to a working mother who is also a single parent and must work full-time.

Don't try to do everything at once. Working mothers who have too much to do and just can't get everything right need to set priorities: do what's most important first, and, if you can't do everything, simply let some things go by the board. If you can't get the dishes done, set your hair, and get to a PTA meeting all by seven o'clock, arrange to go to the PTA meeting; that's important to your child. Then decide whether it's more important to do the dishes or set your hair. Whichever you choose, don't feel guilty. Your child won't be hurt by unset hair or a few dishes in the sink.

Betty Friedan has described enthusiastically a working arrangement known as "flextime" that has been used in this country as one solution to the rigidity of the American workplace.[5] Flextime, which is used by a number of American businesses today, is designed so that everyone works during the midday core of hours but allows starting, leaving, and lunch times to vary according to individual needs. Some individuals working on flextime start work later than others so they can drop their children off at day care centers. Others decide to skip lunch hour and leave at three o'clock in the afternoon in order to be home when the children come home from school. (Flextime may become more available if more women enter the work force and if more businesses vie for them. Today, however, it is still a solution only for a small number of people working in businesses where it is operating.)

Be sure to provide good surrogate care. Baby sitters and other alternative caregivers may serve as satisfactory mother-surrogates, especially when children are very young. But they must do good jobs of fulfilling their roles if children are to adjust satisfactorily to the loss of their mothers for a number of hours a day.[6]

Remember, the TV set is not a satisfactory baby sitter!

Communicate clearly to your children the advantages of your entering the work force. They need to know that you are going off because you want to provide something useful to the family, and not because their needs are unimportant.

Finally, find time no matter what to give your child love, attention, and understanding. No surrogate mother can provide your love. Remember, it is not the amount of time that you spend with your children that is important. It is the *quality* of the time. Use your time well: know and love your children and let them know and love you.

HELP: WHAT DO I DO NOW?

A Case Study Involving Divorce

I. Identification and Sources of Information

Name: Wally Harper
Address: 413 Sunset Road, Silverton, Ohio
Age: Eight years
Sources of Information:

1. Personal observation
2. Interview with Wally's parents
3. Interview with Wally's therapist

II. Family History

Wally is the only child of Lydia and Bob Harper. Mr. Harper is a physical education instructor at Silverton High School; his mother was unemployed until their divorce last year, and currently works as a legal secretary for a firm in Silverton.

Mr. and Mrs. Harper were married three years before Wally was born. The marriage was a stormy one, especially after Wally's birth, and was characterized by bitter fights over money and several separations.

Wally was born after an uncomplicated delivery. His parents report no noticeable problems in his early years. When Wally was six years old, his father left home after a violent fight with his mother and didn't return. Mrs. Harper was despondent and spent large portions of her time in bed for several months following the separation. Mr. Harper visited the house occasionally to see Wally but usually stayed for only a short time. Most visits ended in verbal battles between parents. When Mr. Harper filed for divorce six months later, Mrs. Harper did not contest it.

III. Case History

Wally was first noticed as a behavior problem about the time the divorce was finalized. He had always been a bedwetter, but at this point he began to have daytime accidents as well. Although he had been a good student in first grade, he began to have difficulty doing the most simple reading and writing. He began to scribble in his coloring books, although he was able to write his name clearly on the bedroom walls with crayons. (His mother spanked him for this misdeed.)

At the end of first grade, his teacher suggested that he was not ready to enter second grade. First of all, she told his mother, he hadn't learned the basic skills. Second, he acted out in class and was disruptive to the other students. She suggested that Wally repeat the grade or be sent to a special education class.

Mrs. Harper called her husband for help. She thought that Wally probably ought to go to the special class. Mr. Harper disagreed.

"I won't have any son of mine in a class for crazy kids!" he yelled.

Wally watched the scene silently. Later he wet his pants.

In the fall, he began the special education program.

At the same time Wally began studying in the special education class, Mrs. Harper began her full-time job. Wally was instructed to go to a neighbor's house after school and stay there until five o'clock when his mother came home. Wally was permitted to stay at the neighbor's for only a month, however, because he began to bully the smaller children in the household. After that, he became a "latchkey kid." His mother put the house key around his neck on a chain. Wally was told to come right home and to stay in the house until she got there. Usually, he spent the time watching TV.

One day Mrs. Harper came home and found that Wally had broken all the dishes in the kitchen. She was horrified.

> **Mrs. Harper** (screaming): How could you do such a terrible thing?
> **Wally:** I don't know.
> **Mrs. Harper:** You most certainly *do* know! Why?
> **Wally:** I don't know.
> **Mrs. Harper:** Can't you understand what you've done? Don't

you realize? Those dishes were good ones. It would take me
two days' work to buy more like them!

Wally: I don't care

Mrs. Harper: What's wrong with you? Do you hate me like your
father does? What am I supposed to do with you?

Wally: (Looks down at floor; says nothing.)

The next day Mrs. Harper made an appointment to see a child
psychologist. At first Mr. Harper refused to be involved, saying that
he didn't think Wally needed anything but a good spanking and that
if Mrs. Harper would attend more effectively to Wally, he'd be all
right. Later Mr. Harper agreed to attend some of the sessions.

The therapist suggested family therapy in which both parents and
Wally met with the therapist, sometimes separately and sometimes
together.

He worked with Mr. and Mrs. Harper on developing a relationship that would help Wally, and together they formulated rules of
discipline and came to agreement on matters such as visitation rights
and so on.

He explained to both of them that Wally's behavior both at school
and at home represented an attempt to regress to an earlier period
in which Wally pretended that everything was OK. It was also an
attempt to get attention from two parents who were so wrapped up
in their own problems that they didn't seem to be aware of Wally's.

IV. Present Status, Diagnosis, and Prognosis

At the moment, Wally is a very upset little boy who will need a lot
of help from both his parents and his therapist if he is to adjust to
his new life. For the time being, Wally's parents have agreed to
have his mother change her working hours to part-time. Wally's
father agreed to pay additional alimony for awhile until they both
felt Wally was strong enough psychologically to be able to have her
away for eight hours per day. Mrs. Harper comes home from work
now before Wally gets out of school, and has begun spending more
time helping Wally with his school work and just playing with him.
The parents have agreed to stop fighting over visitation, and Mr.

Harper has arranged to have Wally visit his new apartment every other weekend.

All of these steps represent good progress toward a solution to Wally's problems. If they continue working with the therapist and work out the personal problems that are still plaguing them both, Mr. and Mrs. Harper will be able to give Wally the help and understanding he needs. In the meantime, he probably will continue to need the extra attention provided by a special education class. Eventually, Wally probably will be able to return to a regular class. His IQ is above normal, and there seems to be no reason for him not to succeed in school once he is able to resolve his adjustment problems.

CHAPTER 7

When You Have Lost Control: Some Help for Parents of Adolescents

Most discipline problems described so far deal with situations in which eventually parents succeed in teaching and children succeed in learning. It would be wonderful if this were the way that lessons in discipline always ended. Unfortunately, that's not the case. Sometimes, no matter what parents do, their children seem determined to embark on dangerous activities.

Why do parents sometimes lose control? One reason is that parents often become afraid and therefore become too inconsistent to discipline effectively. One example given earlier is the child who throws a temper tantrum in order to make her parents buy her ice cream, and who learns that she can get them to give in if she throws the tantrum in a public place. In this case, the child was successfully controlling her parents' behavior instead of the other way around. Another example is the adolescent who threatens to run away from home if he isn't allowed to stay out overnight, and whose parents give in out of fear even when they realize that it would be far better to require him to come home at curfew time.

Another way that parents can lose control is when they disagree with one another about how to handle a given situation. In this case, children learn that they can go to the other parent if the first parent says "no."

Sometimes children are able to manipulate parental behavior because there isn't sufficient communications between parents. In this case, the child might deliberately go first to the mother and then separately to the father, being careful not to bring the issue up when both parents are present at the same time.

> **Child:** Mom, is it OK for me to stay overnight at Janey's house?
> **Mother:** Well, I don't think it's a good idea. Did you do all your homework? What does your Dad say? (The child doesn't answer, but goes directly to her father.)
> **Child** (later): Dad, is it OK for me to go to Janey's house?
> **Father:** Are you sure it's a good idea? You have school tomorrow.
> **Child:** Well, Mom thinks it's OK.
> **Father:** Well, OK then.

When parents are trying to stop their children from whining or nagging, or stop them from playing one parent against the other, they can often solve the problem by using the rules outlined in Chapter 5.

In the first situation, the best solution would be to take care to be consistent and to avoid rewarding any whining, even if it keeps them from doing what they want for a while. Sometimes parents have to stop everything they're doing. Sometimes they have to listen to the whining for a long time before it stops. But without being very careful to not ever let whining children get what they want, whining just won't stop.

In the second situation, the best solution is to establish clear communication with one another, agree on the establishment of all rules, and stick to them when you know you're right.

Parents also lose control when the rewards they are using with their children lose their potency, and their children's behavior comes under the control of outside rewards. Loss of parental control occurs gradually and begins most frequently as children reach early adolescence—the middle school years. By the time children reach high school, so much of their behavior is affected by peer rewards or other outside influences that it can be extremely difficult for parents to find ways to influence them.

Sometimes children become totally disinterested in rewards available to them from either peers or family and seem to be operating on some level unrelated to the real world around them. When this happens, parents may need to get outside professional help. (see Chapter 9).

SPECIAL ADOLESCENT PROBLEM BEHAVIORS

By far the most difficult time for most American parents occurs when children reach the age at which they begin to have freedom to go where they want, be with people they choose themselves, and do what they want. It is at this period of life that children may become involved in a variety of behaviors that their parents don't approve of, including delinquent behaviors of all sorts, use of alcohol or illicit drugs, and sometimes dropping out of school. It's important to realize that no adolescents are totally immune. Problem behaviors of this sort occur among all socioeconomic and social classes.

Adolescents can be arrested by the police for what are known as "status offenses" as well as behaviors that would be delinquent at any age. Status offenses are behaviors that are judged delinquent by virtue of the child's age, and would not be considered criminal if performed by an adult. Two examples are being truant from school and running away from home.

Finally, adolescents are beginning to reach their physical primes and develop an increasing interest in sexuality. Many begin to engage in sexual experimentation, which can lead to trouble if not handled properly.

Characteristics of Adolescence That Make Problem Behavior Likely

Parents of adolescents the world over tend to agree that adolescence is just awful! Adolescents themselves usually agree. Adolescents often upset their parents because they're inconsistent, irresponsible, noisy, or rude. And they are no more happy with their parents than their parents are with them: they point out that their parents never understand what's going on. As one teenager put it, "It seems as if my Mom grew up in the Dark Ages. Talking to her is like talking to a dusty history book. Sometimes I wonder if she ever was a kid herself. I tend to doubt it."

Psychologists point out that many of the tensions of this age period are related to real physiological changes and the psychological concomitants of these changes. They also point out that many parents exacerbate the situation by placing extra stress on children at this time, and also by vacillating between different expectations they have for them.[1] The parent who nags her son to do his homework instead of going to the ball game with his friends perhaps has forgotten how important school activities such as ball games were to her when she was fifteen. The parent who tells a sixteen-year-old on Monday that he's just not mature enough to take the family car out at night, and then on Tuesday tells him that he ought to begin acting like an adult and take some responsibility around the house is setting the scene for trouble.

The problem is that many parents are ambivalent about their adolescent children. On the one hand, they want them to grow up and become mature adults. On the other hand, they're not ready to let go yet and really would like to keep their children younger. When this ambivalence leads to inconsistent behavior that the adolescent doesn't really know how to deal with, the result is often conflict.

*Special psychological characteristics of adolescence.** Many psychologists have described adolescence.[2] Children at this period are characterized primarily by a great deal of anxiety about most things in their lives. Their sudden increased physical growth rate startles them. The high variability of growth rates among children of the same age makes adolescents supersensitive about their appearances. Peers begin to play major roles in what adolescents do with their

---

*This is an extremely brief description of one of the most complicated and confusing stages of human development. If you are the parent of an adolescent, you probably will want to read a review of the stage given in the chart in Chapter 9 and follow it up with one of the books on adolescence described in Chapter 10.

time. When peer values conflict with parental values, trouble develops.

Adolescents are just beginning to understand the changes they must make in their lives before they can become adults. These changes are often frightening: life becomes a series of conflicting possibilities. Should the adolescent be preparing for college? What should she study? Should she be preparing for an office job? What does she *want* to be as an adult? What is she *able* to be? What are the realities? As a result, the adolescent often vacillates (in ways that can infuriate parents) from adult status to child status and back again.

One mother put it this way: "Phil is fifteen years old going on eight; I never know from day to day how old to expect him to be."

The vacillating behavior of adolescents, their insecurities, and their fears about what lies ahead are very important for parents to understand if they are to help their children through this period.

DELINQUENT BEHAVIORS

The most common form of delinquent behavior among middle school and high school students is habitual disobedience.

Habitual Disagreement and Disobedience

Mrs. Allison tells her sixteen-year-old son Bobby that he can't go out to watch TV at his friend's house until he finishes his homework assignment. Bobby sullenly responds, "Bug off, Ma," grabs his jacket, and slams the door as he leaves. He doesn't bother coming home until midnight.

Alice Allison, aged fourteen, doesn't leave the house, but she doesn't like what her mother cooked for supper. "I'm not going to eat any of this shit," she tells her mother, and she gets a TV dinner out of the freezer.

Her mother remonstrates with her. But Alice doesn't bother to respond and takes her TV dinner to her room. Her mother doesn't even bother to ask Alice to do the dishes because she's too tired to listen to more verbal abuse.

How to help. Mrs. Allison has lost control. She, like other parents, can regain it only if she's not too afraid of her children to try. One solution to loss of control that has worked for some families is to establish a family council and to make a contract with the children that specifies just what rewards they will get for behaving in satisfactory ways. If this solution is to work, the children must know without doubt that they will lose these rewards for continued disobedience. If Bobby and Alice Allison learned that there are definite advantages to behaving properly they would be far less likely to disobey. Mrs. Allison might decide, for example, that Bobby can use the family car on weekends only if he shapes up, does his homework, and speaks politely. In similar fashion, she might decide that if Alice doesn't like what has been prepared for dinner, she will have to go without eating. In this case, Mrs. Allison will have to make sure that TV dinners or other alternatives just aren't available.

Vandalism

Did you ever stop to wonder who wrote the graffiti on the walls of the rest room at your local movie theatre? It probably was an early adolescent. Another common delinquent behavior among early adolescents is more serious vandalism. The possibilities are enormous. Newspapers frequently describe situations in which children break into a school and damage classrooms, spraypaint walls of schools and other buildings, cherrybomb mailboxes, break lightbulbs in buildings, or shoot out street lights.

Who commits these acts? For the most part, they are middle schoolers, not high schoolers. They are almost always in a group when they engage in these activities. And, surprisingly to many parents, they come as often from middle-class backgrounds these days as from other social classes. One study of school-age vandalism showed that half the population of middle-class children below tenth grade who were interviewed admitted to at least one act of vandalism during the past year. Even more surprising to many is that girls of this age tend to enjoy these activities more than boys.[3]

Why do children vandalize? Many early adolescents who are caught report that they did it out of anger—toward their parents, the school, or their teachers. It's not simply anger that causes vandalism, though. It's camaraderie. Children vandalize in groups because it's fun and because they receive a great deal of reward from their peers for engaging in dangerous behavior.

"It's fun mostly when there's just a little chance of getting caught," one fourteen-year-old girl explained. "We took the spray cans and wrote dirty words in red, white, and blue on the post office wall . . . then we threw the cans away and slowly walked back when the policeman came by. We wanted to see his face. Two of the kids didn't come back with us. I guess they were more afraid than we were. They didn't go with us the next time either."

There's less chance of getting caught writing obscenities on the walls of toilet booths than there is spraypainting the front of the post office. Possibly the children who were most frightened expressed their feelings in the privacy of toilet booths the next time.

How to help. You have just discovered that your child, who has never been in trouble before, was one of a group who knocked over your neighbor's garbage can. What should you do? The first thing is to discover why your child did such a thing.

First off, don't begin by punishing. Begin by talking . . . and listening. Why did your daughter do this? Is she angry? Why? At whom? Listen and don't judge. Let her know you understand if she has feelings of hostility. Help her to express her hostile feelings verbally. She'll get into a lot less trouble if she can do this with you than if she continues acting out.

What if your daughter knocked over the garbage can simply because the other kids told her to do it? In this case, you have a different kind of problem. Peer pressure is extremely important to this age group, and you will have to do your best to combat it with moral reasoning. Discuss the damage that was done, and ask her how she thinks your neighbor felt, and how she would feel if someone were to vandalize her property. You can be successful with this approach if: (1) your child is able to empathize and has already learned from you the importance of behaving in moral ways; and (2) you have developed a warm, understanding, and communicative relationship with one another.

Truancy

Truancy is a status offense; the habitual truant may get into trouble not only with the school authorities but also with outside legal authorities. The habitual truant usually begins by cutting classes. Once he starts, it becomes more and more difficult for him to return to face the teacher. As he falls behind in his school work, attendance becomes more punitive. He has to face the music, take the lowered grade, and suffer the indignity of teacher criticism. Eventually the class-cutter decides that the best thing to do is to stay away from school altogether. For him, the immediate reward of hanging out with his friends at the corner drugstore or going joy riding in a friend's car is far preferable to facing the punishment of returning to school and angry teachers.

A great deal has been written about the large number of youths from low socioeconomic backgrounds who fail in school and reduce their frustrations by truancy.[4] But sometimes students with average or above average grades also get caught in this vicious circle. The first time they cut, it is just a lark. Perhaps their friends dared them to cut; perhaps they cut because they are unprepared for a test. But returning to class for these youngsters turns out to be harder than they expected. They are afraid to face the teacher and aren't sure just what to say. They haven't picked up the new assignment and have gotten further behind than they expected. As a result, they cut again.

One middle-class mother reported her horror at receiving a call from the high school counselor. Her fifteen-year-old son had not been to school for two weeks!

"I got up every morning and made a hot breakfast for Jim," she reported. "He always got up on time, talked with me about what he was going to do at school that day, and took off in time to be there for homeroom period. I just can't imagine what happened, where he's been going, or what's going on!"

When her son came home that afternoon, his mother confronted him.

> **Mother:** Well, Jim, how was your day?
> **Jim:** OK . . . same as usual.

Mother: How was math class?

Jim: OK, I guess. There was a quiz.

Mother: Jim, I got a phone call from Mr. Thomas this morning. He says you weren't at school today. He says you haven't been there for the last two weeks.

Jim: Uhh!

Mother: What's going on?

Jim: I don't know.

Mother: Where have you been?

Jim: Nowhere.

Mother: Nowhere?

Jim: Well, I've been going to the luncheonette and having coffee.

Mother: Alone?

Jim: No, with a couple of kids.

Mother: Who?

Jim: Oh, Billy, Chuck, Sam, and some other guys you don't know.

Mother: All day?

Jim: No, most of the day. Sometimes we rode around in Sam's car.

Mother: What else were you doing?

Jim: Nothing.

Mother: Pot?

Jim: Yeah, a little . . . but not much.

Mother: Anything else?

Jim: No.

Mother: Why?

Jim (Pause): I don't know, Ma. Really, I don't know.

Jim and his mother talked a long time that afternoon. Jim didn't seem to know why he had been truant. He knew that he had not been enjoying classes for some time. He felt that the teachers were out to get him, and that nothing he seemed to be doing was right. When Chuck had suggested one morning that they head for the luncheonette instead of the high school, he went along without thinking much about it. He knew kids did it all the time and thought he'd just forge his father's signature on an excuse. It wouldn't be too hard. But then they did it the next day. And then the next.

They never talked about the consequences. Jim was afraid to go back to class. He was terribly afraid about what was going to happen to him. He had wanted to go to college, and he thought he had blown his chances.

When Jim's father came home that evening, the family had a conference. They decided that they all should meet with Jim's counselor and see how they could pull the pieces together.

This family succeeded in working out the problem. The counselor was glad to help, particularly since it was the first time Jim had ever been in trouble. The teachers gave Jim a second chance, and Jim stayed home every afternoon for several weeks catching up on back homework. In addition, Jim's parents arranged for outside help. In this case, they consulted a family therapist who helped both Jim and his parents learn to talk with one another, and, most importantly, express their feelings. It took awhile for Jim to understand why he felt as unhappy as he did in school. When he understood that his teachers were really interested in his success and not trying to "get" him, he began to do better school work. His teachers were careful to let him know they approved of his effort, and his parents rewarded him by approving strongly. Jim eventually began to find school much more fun.

It is not always so simple, of course. Sometimes truant children miss so much school that it is impossible for them to catch up; sometimes their reasons for cutting in the first place have to do with a history of failure from the early years of school. When this happens, some families find that schools with alternative curricula that allow children to go at their own pace and provide extra assistance can be helpful. Many alternative schools have opened in the past decade; most are private, although public schools in some cities offer alternatives for children who seem to need them.

How to help. The first thing that parents can do in helping a child who has been truant is to make sure they are communicating with their child. If you are there when your child goes off to school and when he comes home, you are more likely to know what he's been up to than if you are never around or don't talk with him. Sometimes, even when parents are there, children like Jim may hide their bad behavior successfully. If your child succeeds in keeping something from you, don't feel that you are a bad parent and let your guilt impede your disciplining. Start with what you have and begin communicating. Remember, a child who is truant is usually one who is not happy. Punishing without taking the time to find out what the real issues are may lead only to more unhappiness. The best role you can play is that of a loving supporter. Help your child to talk about what is bothering him at school. Remember, the truancy will supply its own punishment independent of what you do or say. Your child may need your help through the difficult steps he must take to deal with the punishment. He needs your understanding.

Running Away

Running away from home is another status offense. Some of the reasons that runaways give for leaving home are feelings of alienation, school problems, or what they perceive rightly or wrongly as parental abuse. Often runaways are children whose behavior has been out of control at home for a long time and who feel that their parents simply don't understand them. Sometimes runaways leave home to demonstrate to their parents that they are grown up enough to get along without them. Unfortunately, they are usually wrong.

Runaways face serious dangers when they leave home. Usually they have no money or work skills. They begin often by hitchhiking to other cities, and this is just the start of the trouble. Police reports are full of attacks and rapes of young hitchhikers. Once they reach their destinations, these adolescents are unable to support themselves in legal jobs, which makes them easy targets for unscrupulous adults; many young boys and girls quickly find themselves turning to prostitution or drug dealing. Their number, however, has never been adequately estimated since arrest and juvenile court statistics do not include those who don't get caught.

How to help. The best thing to do, of course, is to provide a home environment in which children feel they want to stay. This means being understanding and willing to listen and to establish rules for coexistence. It also means educating children as to the dangers of leaving home without adequate protection. Children need to be made aware of just what they're liable to get into if they do decide that leaving home is better than staying and trying to work out the problems that exist there.

Sometimes, even when parents do their best, children leave. When this happens, it's important to keep lines of communication open, and to be ready to listen if a call comes.

What if your child runs away and comes back? The first thing to do is determine why she left in the first place. Often she will tell you that you were just too strict; she wants a freer environment. At this point, you need to make a plan. The new relationship you want to build must be reasonable not only for your child but for you, too. Plan a family conference and establish a contract. Maybe you feel that she should be home every night by eleven. She wants to be free to come and go as she sees fit and to stay out all night if she wants. Compromise if you must—maybe setting a curfew of midnight. But be sure that you clearly specify all the rules in your contract, as well as the benefits received if the rules are followed. If your daughter comes in on time, she is entitled to her allowance (or whatever); if not, she is not rewarded. If the rules and consequences are established, and agreed upon by all parties, there will no longer be reason for arguments.

Sometimes disagreements between adolescents and their parents run so deep that it's impossible to set up a contract that everyone can agree to. When this happens, it's time to call for outside professional help. Family therapy is often the most successful approach to this type of problem. The therapist's job is to show both the adolescent and the parents just what messages each is communicating to the other, and to help everyone understand the situation from the other points of view.

Drug and Alcohol Abuse

Among all segments of our population, drug and alcohol use among teenagers is on the rise; alcoholism and drug addiction are frequent problems. Common drugs available to children from elementary school on include marijuana (pot or grass); barbiturates (yellow jackets or blue devils); amphetamines (bennies); LSD (acid); methaqualone (quaaludes); and even heroin (horse or smack) and cocaine (coke). Heroin, barbiturates, and methaqualone all have the potential of physical dependence and physical addiction. All have the possibility of some of the following adverse side effects: depression, paranoic symptoms, hallucinations, toxic psychosis, panic reactions, and loss of appetite.[5]

Drug use is most often a group affair: children usually begin with marijuana at a party or somewhere with a number of peers. Peer approval is a major reward at first. Later, adolescents report that they use the drugs to get feelings of euphoria, relaxation, anxiety reduction, exhilaration, and distortion of senses. By the time teenagers or younger children begin to use hard drugs, they often do it without needing the reinforcement of peers.

Alcohol use is even more common than is drug use among American adolescents. Researchers interviewing students in a variety of New York state high schools found that over 80 percent of the students admitted that they drank; 23 percent of a national sample of sixteen- to eighteen-year-olds admitted to being drunk at least four or five times.[6]

Why do American adolescents get involved with drugs or alcohol? In many cases they're just trying to be more grown up. Three-quarters of all adults in this country drink alcohol, and one-tenth are problem drinkers. It's not surprising that young adolescents imitate them.

A related factor is the attraction supplied by the media. People who drink are consistently portrayed as popular, beautiful, and sophisticated. The message conveyed is that the youngster will be equally appealing if he or she drinks.

The desire to keep up with peers—to be one of the gang—is another reason.

Marilyn, an attractive thirteen-year-old from an upper-middle-class neighborhood in Cleveland, is a case in point.

I guess I started using drugs because I wanted to be like the other kids in class, and because I wanted to impress my boyfriend. All the older kids were using drugs, and we all wanted to see what it was like. First I messed around with pills and pot. Later, my boyfriend got hold of some smack at a party. I snorted a couple of times, skinned a lot, and, after that, I mained it. I stopped going to school. After awhile, my mother caught me stealing silverware from the house to sell it and my folks sent me to a special school for kids who are emotionally disturbed. But it was easier for me to get heroin there than out on the streets. All the other kids got it from their friends, and we shared. Looking back, I'm not sure I would have had any friends if I hadn't used drugs. Everybody was doing it, and I wanted to be like everyone else. My parents never spoke to me once about drugs before I started. Not even after I started. I guess they tried to pretend they didn't know. I used to go and tell my mother what I did. I guess I kinda hoped she'd make me stop. But she didn't.

Phil started on marijuana at thirteen, and went through LSD and amphetamines before getting into heroin at fifteen. Phil's father is a successful surgeon, but Phil never completed high school once he started his habit.

I started on smack exactly on the third anniversary of the first time I smoked pot. I was really scared. I'd never stuck a needle in my arm before, for one thing. I did it in the beginning because the other kids were doing it. But once I started, it was a thrill thing with me. I stopped school. It's not the same high with smack that it is with bennies. It's the wild rush for the first minute, that's what it is. After that it's good, but it's never the same as that first minute. As soon as it starts wearing off, you get a sick kind of feeling wondering how you'll get more. I want to stay off because I saw such messes from it. One girlfriend of mine died from hepatitis. I used to main it with her—I never knew why I was so lucky I didn't get it. Another kid I know landed up in the hospital with a $100-a-day habit. Everytime you stick that needle in, you're playing with your life.

Most drug users like Marilyn and Phil have one characteristic in common: they tend to have low self-concepts and feel distressed much of the time when they're not high. Being high gives them a feeling of euphoria and a chance to forget their other problems. Marilyn felt she needed to start using drugs because her boyfriend would like her if she did; Phil enjoyed the highs he got from heroin because they helped him forget how low he felt at school. Marilyn wanted help from her parents in controlling her behavior, but she didn't get it. Phil's father was too busy to be aware of what his son was into until it was too late.

How to help. First, don't push the panic button. It's important to realize that experimentation does not necessarily lead to serious problems such as those of Marilyn and Phil, if you provide help early enough. Many children try out pot or a gin and tonic and find that it's something they just don't want to do anymore, regardless of what the other kids are doing.

Usually when youngsters use drugs or alcohol a great deal they are having difficulty coping in many areas of their lives. Many report feelings of alienation from their parents and friends and lack of authentic, meaningful relationships. Many are terrified of becoming independent adults. It's these children who need help—both in breaking their drug habits and in solving the other problems that made it easier for them to enjoy drugs in the first place.

Second, it's important to recognize the symptoms of alcoholism and addiction. These include falling school grades, shortened attention span, absences from school and truancy, irritability, impulsive behavior, lying, inability to cope with frustration, and, often, decreases in physical coordination skills.[7]

Once you have diagnosed the problem, you can take the following steps:

1. Establish concern. Show your love as well as your concern over what you see.
2. Point out exactly what changes you can see in your child.
3. Be consistent and don't accept excuses. Alcoholics and addicts

often develop excuses and rationalizations to avoid admitting the problem. Don't fall for it.

4. Confront the problem and do not condone it. Remember, it is possible to reject the alcoholism or addiction and at the same time accept your child. Be as loving as you can.
5. By all means, if your child is using drugs and doesn't stop, seek outside professional help.

ADOLESCENT SEXUAL ACTIVITY

Sexual expression in our society is increasingly free among both adults and children. Just as parents and the media serve as models for adolescents in drinking and sometimes in drug use, parents and the media teach that being sexy and acting sexy is the sophisticated way to behave and will lead to popularity.

Sigmund Freud referred to the period from puberty on as the "genital stage." During this period, hormonal changes in the body increase sexual urges. One activity common to teenagers increasingly interested in their genitals is masturbation. Whether parents realize it or not, almost all teenagers masturbate and almost all males masturbate to orgasm. In addition, increasing numbers of teenage boys and girls each year experiment with sexual intercourse. This is true not just of high school students but increasingly of middle school students as well. About one-fifth of thirteen- and fourteen-year-olds admit to having had sexual intercourse. Researchers believe that many more have had intercourse but don't admit it to interviewers. It is estimated that four million teenage girls and six million boys are sexually experienced.[8]

One reason for earlier sexual activity is that children mature sexually sooner than they used to. The reason for this, according to physicians, is that children today are better nourished and healthier. Today the average age of menstruation is only 12.5 years, about five years younger than a century ago. The problem is that while some twelve-year-olds may be physically capable of having intercourse and becoming pregnant, they usually aren't psychologically capable of dealing with the resulting problems.

Another reason that youngsters become sexually experienced at such early ages is peer pressure. What friends think of them is very important to young adolescents. When the peer group rewards early sexual experience, it is difficult for young adolescents to ignore the pressure.

Pregnancy

The pregnancy rate among adolescents of all socioeconomic backgrounds in this country is on the increase. Each year some 30,000 girls under fifteen become pregnant. One reason, according to researchers, is that many teenagers simply don't have an accurate understanding about the time of greatest risk. Another reason is that some kids don't know why pregnancy occurs!

Lack of knowledge about sexuality leads teenagers to offer explanations such as the following for why they thought they'd never get pregnant: "I thought if you had sex on Sunday, you'd never get pregnant." . . . "He said I had to be seventeen to get pregnant." . . . "If you have sex standing up, it's hard to become pregnant." . . . "If you dance around after intercourse, it's almost impossible to get pregnant."[9]

It might seem difficult to understand why so many young girls become pregnant, given the wide availability of contraception. However, the fact is that many teenagers are afraid to ask for information. Many don't use birth control when it is available because they don't want to admit to sex. Many teenagers just beginning sexual exploration tend to have erratic, infrequent, and spontaneous sexual encounters that do not lend themselves easily to birth control. Finally, many teenagers are held back from obtaining adequate information because of feelings of guilt.

The price is high: increased infant mortality, pregnancy complications, and chances of maternal mortality with mothers of such young ages; increased risk of postpartum psychiatric symptoms and attempted suicide; permanent disruption of education; decreased economic opportunity; stigma; and increased divorce rate.

How to help. For one thing, it's terribly important to provide adequate sex education either at home or in school. For sex education to be effective, it must be provided *before* heterosexual activities begin—one important reason that many educators today are promoting sex education in middle school or earlier.

The problem of dealing with sexuality is not unique to Americans. Many countries dealing with the problem have made the decision to teach sex education in the schools. In some countries, such as Denmark, Sweden, Czechoslovakia, and East Germany, sex education is compulsory. In the United States, where curriculum control lies within each school district, we have no national program. Most psychologists believe that too few American schools offer sex education. And when they do offer it, they don't explore the students' feelings about sexuality. Discussion of sexual values—whether it takes place at home or at school—is at least as important in sex education as explanations of the physiology of sexuality and hygiene.

In order to help teenagers feel free to discuss their developing sexuality and what it means to them, parents need to be free themselves in their own discussion. Parents who are stand-offish and who do not provide either the information or the support that their children are looking for are likely to have children who get their information from peers. Too often, this information is not accurate.

Finally, parents need to remember that they are very important models for their children when it comes to sexual behavior. Single parents, especially, need to be aware of just what they're teaching their teenage children and make sure that it's what they want their children to learn. Teenagers won't buy the argument that "it's OK for me to have my boyfriend (or girlfriend) over to spend the night and have sexual relations, but not for you."

Sexually Transmitted Diseases

Along with pregnancy, there has been an increase in the incidence of sexually transmitted diseases among both high school and middle school students in America. Teenagers account for about 25 percent of the one million cases of gonorrhea and herpes reported annually. The cause of these diseases is, like that of most pregnancies, ignorance. Teenagers often are not aware of either the physical causes or the long- or short-term symptoms of the diseases. Most are unaware of methods to protect themselves. And most are uncomfortable discussing the problem. The price of sexually transmitted disease among young adolescents, like that of pregnancy, is high: long-term serious illness, and increased infant mortality and pregnancy complications if girls become pregnant.

How to help. Many of the same steps designed to reduce teenage pregnancy can help in dealing with the dangers of sexually transmitted diseases. Youngsters need to be educated, whether they receive this education at home or at school. Parents need to be warm and supportive so that their children aren't afraid to ask what is on their minds. They need to know a lot about their children's feelings. This knowledge comes most easily when parents take time to be with their children. Finally, parents need to realize that if their teenager comes home with a sexual problem—whether it involves pregnancy or disease—the way to begin is *not* to become angry. The way to begin is to provide love, understanding, and help.

CHAPTER 8

When Child Abuse Becomes a Danger

The first seven chapters of *Discipline Is Not a Dirty Word!* dealt with different ways that parents can teach children skills and behaviors that will be useful to them as adults and that, in many cases, will make them easier to live with until that time.

Most of the discipline measures consist of ways to increase good behavior through reward, loving attention, understanding, and being a good model. Sometimes none of these methods work. When all else fails, as Chapter 3 points out, it may be time to punish.

When parents try to change their children's behavior by doing something unpleasant, we call it punishment. A spanking is a punishment. So is a slap on the hand. There are, in addition, many kinds of punishment that don't involve anything physical. Some of the more common kinds used by parents when they can't get their children to do what they want include ridicule, sarcasm, and humiliation. Physical incarceration—as, for example, locking a child in his room—is still another example of a punishment designed to teach.

Chapter 3 pointed out that punishment does the job sometimes—when children are able to escape the punishment by being good and when it is not too severe or too frequent. When children can't escape and when punishment is too harsh, we call it abuse.

DISCIPLINE DOESN'T MEAN ABUSE!

Abuse is not discipline: it doesn't teach good behavior. Child abuse means doing physical harm to children. It also means doing psychological harm.

Child abuse is as old as human society. However, since child abuse is rarely reported and easily covered up, it has been difficult to assess its frequency—at least until recently. Today, however, the mass media have drawn attention to the problem. This fact, together with the use of medical technology that allows physicians to measure the extent of old healed fractures and other wounds, has made it increasingly apparent that physical abuse of children is far more prevalent in America than most of us had imagined in the past.

It is estimated that, in this country, six million children per year are victims of child abuse or serious neglect bordering on abuse. More than half of these are children under the age of six. According to statistics, fourteen of every one hundred children suffer physical abuse—from biting, kicking, punching, hitting with an object, or heavy beating.[1] Unfortunately, there are no available statistics on psychologically abused children.

It is not possible to determine whether child abuse is on the rise. It's clear, however, that it exists. Further, it exists among all socioeconomic classes. The abused child may be the slum child; she may also be your next-door neighbor.

Why Child Abusers Abuse

There are many reasons why child abuse occurs. Abusing parents are inadequate to deal with their problems. They may have low self-esteem, for example, that makes it uncomfortable for them to interact with other people. They may not be getting along with their spouses and feel isolated within their families. They may be terribly afraid of being rejected by others and can't cope with their emotions. They may have low frustration tolerances and have too much difficulty controlling themselves to be able to manage their children's behavior effectively. Often abusing parents were abused children.

Sometimes abused children have some special characteristic that sets them off from their siblings and seems to be related to their parents' abuse of them. Some abused children, for example, have physical deformities or are mentally retarded. Some have the misfortune to resemble a hated relative or were the cause of a difficult pregnancy. Usually only one parent inflicts the actual injuries. The other demonstrates his or her inadequacy by not interfering.

The Effects of Child Abuse

Child abuse hurts parents as well as children.

What child abuse does to parents. One way to think of the abusing parent is as a child who has just been pushed beyond his frustration tolerance by a playmate. The playmate has not only won the game of checkers but is going away for the weekend to the beach with his parents. The frustrated child has not only just lost the game but hasn't been invited anywhere with his own parents. In fact, he hasn't even seen his own father in the six months since his parents divorced. All of a sudden he jumps up, knocks the checker set to the floor, pushes his playmate down, and charges out of the room. The playmate gets up; he has no idea what really took place.

What did happen? In this example, this unhappy child's aggression relieved a little of his tension—but only for a few minutes. The problem, as he soon realizes, is that the situation hasn't changed at all: even though he had a brief moment of pleasure knocking down the checker set, the playmate still won the game and is still looking forward to an exciting weekend. And, regardless of his actions, the unhappy child still has no way to arrange a visit with his own father. He hasn't really won anything.

The abusing parent goes through many of the same steps. He is unhappy about something he can't control, and he lashes out at the closest victim to relieve some of the tension. The victim doesn't understand why he is singled out and therefore doesn't learn how to behave so as to avoid the abuse. And the lashing out serves only to increase the parent's own unhappiness because it demonstrates once again that he can't control the situation.

Most abusing parents are unrealistic and demanding of their children. They tend to assume that their child is capable of providing them with what they think they need—adult love and assurance— and they become very angry when they discover that their child simply can't do this.

Some psychologists suggest that one reason that abusing parents have such unreasonable expectations of their children is that they did not receive a sufficient amount of love from their own parents when they were growing up. It's almost as if the parent is seeking from the child the love he never received. The child, however, is helpless. The irony is that the child is dependent on a totally un- dependable person.[2]

Another characteristic of the abusing parent is that he doesn't usually know how to discipline and often confuses discipline with punishment. When punishment doesn't work the first time, he de- cides to increase it the next time. When this doesn't work, the problem—and the stress—accelerate.

What child abuse does to children. Abused children usually have little understanding of why they are being abused. Sadly, they often believe that they deserve what is happening to them. They are weak, helpless, and unable to recognize the inadequacy of their abusing parents. Often they feel it is their duty to protect their parents. An example of this attitude is the child who lies to the authorities for her parents and tells them that her bruises came from falling down the stairs or falling off a bicycle when, in fact, the bruises came from a beating.

When children feel it's their duty to protect abusing parents, it can be difficult for authorities to learn the truth and provide help. One abused child brought to the hospital for the fourth time in one year for serious injuries kept insisting that he was clumsy and just "kept falling off my bike." Authorities investigating the family, however, were able to confirm through neighbors that here was a great deal of fighting in the family and that the boy had been beaten regularly by his father. The boy continued to deny the abuse, how- ever, even though he was confined to the hospital with kidney dam- age from the last beating.

Eventually the mother of this child confirmed the abuse. She admitted to authorities that she was afraid that if she sought help her husband would leave them. At first the boy tried to argue with his mother and stuck to his original statement that he had fallen off his bicycle. Eventually, when confronted with evidence, he broke down and admitted what had happened.

Ironically, this boy had been unwilling to admit the truth because, like his mother, he felt guilty about what had occurred. Only when he was given a great deal of reassurance from therapists did he begin to understand that he was not beaten because he was bad, and that he was not the source of his family's problems.

How Can You Tell If You're an Abusing Parent? A young mother of a two-year-old child was afraid that she was a potential abuser.

"Sometimes when I'm at home with Ronnie, and she's whining, I catch myself clenching my fists. My God! I'm afraid one day I'll fly off the handle and sock the kid! It's so awful being alone in the house with her all day, and listening to her whine and complain. When she slops her food on the table, I feel as if I won't be able to control myself. What if I hurt her?"

This mother was married to a man whose work involved a lot of travel. She was at home alone with her child for four to five days every week.

This mother needed help so that she could be sure she wouldn't do anything that might hurt her child or herself. There are a variety of steps that she might have taken to help solve the problem, for example, joining a Mother's Day Out at her church, taking a class while she left her baby with the sitting service provided there, or simply getting out of the house in some other way where she could talk with other people and get rid of some of her feelings of isolation. She could have joined a support group for first-time mothers or a parenting seminar. She could also have sought counseling to help her deal with her frustrations if getting out of the house didn't do the trick. The important thing was to recognize where the problem lay—within herself—and do something about it.

A father reported that he needed help to keep from hitting his wife and young son. He had been unemployed for the past four months. Standing in the unemployment line was bad enough, he said, but it was worse to come home and have his wife nag him about something she wanted to buy, and then have his six-year-old son try to protect his mother when he went after her.

"Last night, I'm horrified to tell you, I hit my son. And he hadn't done anything at all. It started when Rita asked me why I was so late, as if I was out running around with another woman or something. I lost my temper and told her to go to hell. I guess I slammed my fist hard on the table and that scared the kid. I couldn't stand the scared look on his face, so I yelled to him to get into his own room where he belonged. He didn't move fast enough, so I dragged him by the collar, slapped him hard, and threw him on his bed. I feel so rotten about it today."

This father was upset and frustrated at conditions outside his control. He didn't regularly abuse his family. But when he lost control, he was not sure just what he would do. This father needed professional help in dealing with his frustrations. In his case, family therapy taught him how to communicate his feelings—and his fears—to his wife. Once he was able to let her know how he felt, she was able to give him the understanding he needed. Once she learned what really was on his mind, she worried less about what she couldn't buy. The boy needed to learn that he was safe in his household and that what his father really was angry at had nothing to do with him. None of these things could be learned without some interaction among the three family members. Under the guidance of a professional therapist, group interaction was constructive.

The first of these two examples was not of an abusing parent but of a parent who had sufficient frustrations that she was afraid she might become abusing if she didn't do something to resolve them. The second parent had just crossed the line. The difference between the two is that the second parent was no longer *thinking* about abuse; he was *acting* it out.

A stepmother of two elementary school children reported that she was having a great deal of difficulty with her two new charges. The girls' father had obtained custody after a bitter battle, and he thought that all the family's problems were resolved when this woman had arrived on the scene and married him.

"But I just can't cope with the kids," she complained. "For one thing, they're lazy. No one ever taught them to do anything around the house. They're too lazy even to do their own schoolwork. I can yell at them until I'm blue in the face and it doesn't make a bit of difference. I can even tell them they're stupid and they don't seem to care. I don't think either of them will ever get into college, even with a father who is a physician! They're so lazy, I don't think they even care about that."

This stepmother regularly vented her anger on the two youngsters. She told them in no uncertain terms what she thought of them. One day, when she had just reminded them that they seemed to her to be just like their mother, she became frightened that she had gone too far.

"I know that you can abuse children without beating them," she said. "Am I an abusing parent?"

The answer, unfortunately, was "yes."

The problem for this stepmother and her two stepdaughters, once again, was frustration and the inability to control the situation. This woman did not have any children of her own, and she had expectations of a relationship with her two stepdaughters that was impossible so soon after the divorce and before the girls had adjusted to the trauma of what they thought was their mother's desertion. This stepmother didn't have to beat the girls to abuse them: she attacked where they were most vulnerable—by comparing them with their mother.

The steps needed to correct this situation were more complex than those in the first two examples because the relationships were far more complex. This stepmother eventually worked with a therapist to relieve her own frustrations. The entire family also worked with a family therapist on the complicated relationships that existed among them.

ALL KINDS OF CHILD ABUSE ARE DANGEROUS!

In the three examples given above, adults sought help in solving their problems. What is likely to happen if help is not found? According to statistics gathered by the U.S. Department of Health, Education, and Welfare, at the very least, 2,000 children die annually from abuse, including beatings, burnings, and inadequate care and feeding. But physical abuse is not the only type of abuse that hurts. Many children are seriously psychologically abused. Some children are sexually abused.

With economic problems and unemployment both increasing in the early 1980s, we can expect more parental frustration. Unfortunately this will probably mean greater numbers of abuses of all kinds.

Psychological Abuse

As children grow older and become bigger and stronger, they often learn to fight back. Abusing parents who used to use physical punishment often change their methods at this time. When they lose their ability to win physical battles with their children, they often abuse in psychological ways. The stepmother in the example cited earlier ridiculed her stepdaughters and treated them in ways that lowered their self-esteem and made them feel worthless. If this stepmother hadn't obtained help, her stepdaughters were likely, in turn, to begin to act in worthless ways.

Psychologically abused children usually do poorly in school, exhibit aggressive behavior, and have difficulty getting along with peers and teachers. Parents of such children are often called in to school because their children are disruptive or have learning difficulties. This leads often to further abuse. A vicious cycle often ensues consisting of school-related and behavior problems, parental abuse, and increased aggression in the classroom due to the children's displaced anger toward their parents. Chronic school difficulties increase the abused child's damaged self-esteem.

Psychological abuse is usually designed to change inappropriate behavior to what the parents consider to be socially acceptable ways of responding. The result often is just the opposite of what the parents want.

One fifteen-year-old-girl whose parents were upset by her failing grades was sent to the school psychologist for testing. The psychologist discovered that the girl had an extremely high IQ. The girl, however, did not believe that she was bright. She felt inadequate and incapable of learning. Her grades showed her that she was worthless, as did her parents' obvious disgust. The girl reported to the psychologist that her mother told her regularly that she knew better than to expect her daughter ever to achieve anything . . . that she was just too dumb and too lazy to try.

"And, of course, my Mom was right," the girl told the psychologist. "I can't do anything right—look at the way I've been cutting classes. Sometimes I wonder why it's worth it even to get up in the morning. All I'm going to do is something else stupid."

This girl had simply given up trying—a behavior just the opposite of what her mother had hoped to elicit by her nagging.

Sexual Abuse

Another serious danger to children is sexual abuse. Rape and molestation are, sadly, on the increase. But sexual abuse doesn't have to be rape. It may mean sexual victimization, a term coined to refer to many sexual activities that combine elements of dependency and exploitation, affection and taboo, deception, self-deception, and collusion and that occur as a result of family dysfunction. Incestual sexual relationships fostered by a parent or other relative and characterized by that person as a "secret love relationship" are an example.[3]

Sexual abuse occurs most often in families in which both parents are inadequate to deal with their problems. Abusers tend to be men, usually fathers or stepfathers who look to their children for the companionship and affection they are not receiving from their wives. Often the wife is passive and suffers from medical or physical problems. When she is aware of the abuse, she chooses not to deal with the problem because she is afraid of destroying the relationship she has with the man. As a result, there is no adult in the house to whom the child can turn for help.

The sexual interaction that develops often involves bribing the child and manipulating her need for affection; it does not necessarily require force. Usually it includes fondling or masturbation, which may proceed to intercourse over the years. The results of this relationship, both for the child and for other family members, can be psychologically disastrous. For everyone, it usually involves shame, guilt, and fear. For the child, it leads to serious difficulties later in establishing normal adult sexual and emotional relationships.

Sexual abuse occurs among all socioeconomic and social classes. As discussion of this problem has become more open, parents, children, and teachers are reporting more and more cases of families who need help to deal with the problem.

How do we know that sexual abuse occurs? For one thing, there has been an increase in recent years in the number of elementary school children requiring treatment for sexually transmitted diseases.[4] For another, as the dangers and the incidence of sexual abuse have been publicized by the mass media, more and more children have become less afraid of reporting the situation at home to the authorities. Researchers have found that when children complain to anyone—friends, relatives, or teachers—of sexual abuse, they are usually telling the truth. False complaints are extremely rare.[5]

What should people do if they hear about an incident of sexual abuse? The first step is to report the case to authorities responsible for protecting children. This is required by law in all states. It is also extremely important as one way to reassure the child that she is not trapped in the situation and that she has someone to help her.

Child welfare authorities usually require that families in which they know sexual abuse is occurring receive treatment under court order. Professional therapists working with these families usually take measures to strengthen the relationship between the victim and the nonabusing parent. The child in this case needs to be convinced that she is not responsible, praised for coming forward, and assured that further abuse will not occur. The nonabusing parent needs psychological assistance and support in becoming more assertive and protective.

What happens to the abusing parent who is reported to the authorities? Usually, court orders will require treatment of some kind. Treatment programs vary; many use as their models successful programs for treating drug addiction. In these programs, therapists provide tight structures with rewards and sanctions. Group meetings with other offenders where confrontation of the problem is balanced with psychological support from professional therapists have also been found to be effective.

What Parents Should Do

Are you afraid you might be an abusing parent? Parents who are fearful that they or others in their family are abusing should seek professional help right away. Abuse is serious, and it should be treated that way. If you think you might be an abusing parent, find out just what the cause is and do something about it right away! Don't wait. Your therapist can help you by exploring with you your own feelings, fears, frustrations, and anxieties. But you will need more than this. You will need to learn how to control those frustrations and needs so that you will not harm others in your family. Other family members will probably also need help. For this reason, family therapy can be a successful approach. Another useful approach might be group encounter, in which parents of abused children help each other learn how to control potentially dangerous situations. One word of caution: don't try group therapy without a professional therapist to guide you. You are dealing with a serious problem and need professional advice!

HELP: WHAT DO I DO NOW?
A Case Study Involving Child Abuse

I. Identification and Sources of Information

Name: Katie Anderson
Address: 5478 Sixth Avenue, New York City
Age: Twelve Years
Sources of Information:

1. Interview with Katie
2. Interview with Katie's parents
3. Interview with a psychologist who worked with the family

II. Family History

Katie is the only child of Martha McCarthy and the stepdaughter of Martha's husband, Dave. Katie's parents were divorced when Katie was five years old. Katie's father left the state shortly after the divorce and has not made contact with the family since. He has provided no child support.

Martha and Dave McCarthy were married four years ago and live together with Katie in a two-bedroom apartment. There are no other children in the family, and the McCarthys are not planning to have any more.

Both Martha and Dave are college graduates; Martha works full-time as a secretary; Dave is a salesman for a large manufacturing firm.

Dave reported in an interview that, like many stepfathers, he had looked forward to having a stepdaughter while he had been dating Martha. He liked Katie, and, having no children of his own, initially had wanted to adopt her. Katie, however, had responded with such hostility after the marriage that Dave was shocked. She threatened to run away and find her father, and told Dave in no uncertain terms that she didn't want any part of him, much less a father-daughter relationship.

Martha reported that she, also, had hoped that Katie and Dave would develop a close relationship. Martha was disappointed, but not as upset as Dave was at Katie's hostility. She tried her best to maintain a close relationship with her daughter and pretended as long as she could that she was not aware that a battle was going on between stepfather and stepdaughter.

III. Case History

The first real battle that Katie remembers began when she threatened to leave home to find her father. Before that, Katie remembers being disgusted with her family and wishing she could live elsewhere. She was, however, unprepared for her stepfather's explosion when she announced that she preferred her own father to him.

Dave: Just what the hell do you think you're saying? Your father hasn't given a damn for you since you were a baby! You don't even know him!

Katie: That's not true.

Dave: You're a liar! You know it's true! You're nothing but a cheat and a liar. You think you can hurt me with your crap. Well, you can't!

Katie: I'm not trying to hurt you at all. I couldn't care less what you feel. I don't care anything about you at all.

At that point, Dave's fury was so great that he slapped the girl hard in the face. Martha watched but said nothing. Then she began to cry.

> **Dave:** Now, see what your worthless daughter went and did. She made you cry. I ought to give her a good beating!

Katie ran to her room and hid.

During the next year, according to all three family members, the battles between Dave and Katie escalated. Dave tried to get Katie to admit that he was important to her. Katie stood her ground, and, when she could, hurt him by telling him that her father was better than he was. Dave responded first with hurt feelings and then with increasing bitterness and rage. Increasingly, he punished Katie for hurting him. When verbal punishments had no effect in changing her behavior, he slapped her.

Katie became silent in the house. She spent as little time as she could at home, stayed out often through dinner time, and spent most of the time in her room when she was at home.

Katie's school work began to show the effects of what was happening at home. From an A and B student, she quickly went down to C's. She had wanted to enter a special program for gifted students. Her teachers told her, however, that her grades were too low. She began to cut class frequently, and Mrs. McCarthy received telephone calls from teachers about Katie's acting out behavior in class.

Martha didn't tell Dave about the problem because she was afraid that there would be more battles in the household. At the end of the report card period, however, when Katie brought back two F's, Dave sent her to her room without supper. When she tried to leave the house, he slapped her hard across the face and threatened to lock her in.

> **Dave:** No child of mine is going to act like a moron!
> **Katie:** I'm not your child!
> **Dave:** You're damn well not! You're your father's child! Why don't you go live with him? The two of you are worthy of each other!
> **Katie:** I hate you!

Dave made a charge for Katie, caught the child before she could run out of the room, spread her across his knee, and hit her hard four or five times. He hurt his hand, and badly bruised her buttocks.

Katie hid in her room; Dave cried.

That evening, Dave and Martha decided to seek psychological help. They consulted a therapist, who agreed first to meet with both parents. Then he asked to meet with Katie separately. After several individual sessions, the family began meeting as a group.

IV. Present Status, Diagnosis, and Prognosis

Dave, Martha, and Katie have been in family therapy now for one year. In addition, each family member is in individual therapy.

Dave has spent a great deal of time with the therapist learning about his own feelings concerning his stepdaughter. He now understands why he was so jealous of her father and is working toward developing a new and different kind of relationship with his stepdaughter based on friendship.

Katie has some very strong feelings that she is not yet able to deal with herself. She realizes clearly now that, although she has told Dave many times in the past that she hates him and that she wants to be with her father, the idea of living with her father is really a fantasy. She understands that what she really wanted to do was hurt Dave because she felt that he had taken her mother away from her—she is still having a great deal of difficulty understanding just how much she wanted to hurt him and why. Katie feels guilty about her bad feelings and is still spending much of her time in individual therapy sessions talking about them.

Martha is dealing with her own guilt at allowing the battle between Katie and Dave to go on as long as it did without interfering. She is frightened at what she perceives as her own inability to handle the situation and her own fear of letting the others know what is on her mind.

The three members of this family deal in group therapy sessions with these individual and personal feelings; they are gradually learning how to interact with one another in ways that aren't destructive and how to communicate in ways that others will not perceive as hostile or threatening.

Since therapy began, there have been some fights in the McCarthy household. Dave, however, has refrained from striking Katie, and Katie has refrained from insulting Dave. Katie's school grades have improved, although there still is a great deal more improvement needed if she is ever going to be able to enter the special program for gifted children.

Many more therapy sessions will be required before this family learns to get along without outside help. Nevertheless, the therapist is confident that if all members persevere, there is no reason to believe that they will not succeed eventually.

PART IV

USEFUL INFORMATION
FOR PARENTS

CHAPTER 9

WHAT TO EXPECT OF YOUR CHILD: CHARTS DESCRIBING AGE-RELATED BEHAVIORS

WHAT TO EXPECT OF YOUR CHILD: AGE-RELATED BEHAVIORS

Disciplining means teaching acceptable behavior. Because teaching of any kind requires an understanding of how learners think and solve problems, parents who want to be effective disciplinarians need to understand just how their children think and what to expect of them in different situations and at different ages.

Table 9.1 describes what can be expected of most children as they progress from the preschool years to middle childhood, and from middle childhood through adolescence. The behaviors described for each age level are related to one another in complex ways. For example, a three-year-old who has not yet learned to distinguish himself as separate from the world around him is likely to demonstrate this way of thinking in his language. He will talk about his

Discipline Is Not a Dirty Word

Table 9.1 THE DEVELOPMENT OF SELF-CONCEPTS, EXPECTED BEHAVIORS, AND INTERESTS AND SOCIAL AND FAMILY RELATIONSHIPS OF CHILDREN*

Age (Yrs.)	Self-Concepts	Expected Behaviors	Interests and Social and Family Relationships
2	Egocentric (no real concept of self as separate from others)	No interaction with peers at play Beginnings of parallel play (side by side with others)	Main interest still is learning how to control body and get what is wanted (development of sensorimotor skills) Fears are of imaginary creatures more than real things
3	Beginning first ideas of self as an entity Can't communicate new ideas very well	Describes self in terms of appearances rather than beliefs Enjoys playing make-believe and role-playing to increase ability to understand the world Often can't tell reality from fantasy Begins associative play and imitates others	Beginning to use signs and symbols; will try to use doll as symbol of a baby Interested in communicating with others, although still doesn't understand feelings of others Very interested in toilet training
Preschool Years 4	Getting better idea of self-identity, although still egocentric	Makes morality decisions on basis of reward or punishment	Interested in genitalia and sexual exploration

5	Clearer definition of self shown by increased socialized speech Still self-centered Concept of sexual identity more clear	Solves problems, often by relying on a single aspect Exhibits a great deal of physical and boisterous activity Forms erratic friendships Often dawdles Sexual exploration and masturbation continue	Beginning to explore body and masturbate Beginning cooperative play; leadership patterns developing Speech is increasingly socialized	Less afraid of exploring new situations than before Increasing interest in other children; more interest in children than toys Verbally aggressive but sensitive about being called names Impatient with others Difficulty relating to others Alternately opposes, then makes overtures, toward parents
6	Develops far more clear self-differentiation Judges self-worth in terms of academic success	Is able to solve some problems that were too difficult earlier, but needs concrete objects as help Begins to develop peer friendships that last longer Continues to masturbate—usually in private Has difficulty understanding time concepts	Gradually develops more interest in what parents want and tries to help Continuing interest in genitalia	

Table 9.1 (cont.)

Age (Yrs.)	Self-Concepts	Expected Behaviors	Interests and Social and Family Relationships
7	Judges self increasingly harshly; often ashamed of self	Works and plays in spurts	Increased concern with the reactions of other people in the family
	Less self-centered	Begins to develop close peer friendships	Enjoys humor about sexuality
		Explores sexually, often accompanied by peers	Begins to increase social conformity
		Sensitive	
		Often does not know when to stop in games and interactions with others	
Middle Childhood			
8	Critical of self; self-evaluative	Increasingly outgoing	Not as comfortable with world as before
	Enjoys comparing self with others	Increasingly curious	Has increasing difficulty getting along with family members; poor sibling relationships
		Enjoys school; more persistent and careful with school work	
		Has better perspective of how much can be done	
9	Self-evaluation continues but is less critical	Continues to have close peer friendships	Very involved in personal interests
		Outgoing	Has less difficulty at home with

Age			
	Can admit mistakes without feeling threatened	Curious Social interests sometimes interfere with school work Self-criticism sometimes discourages school work	relationships than before
10	Less self-evaluative More self-satisfied Defines self in terms of thoughts, feelings, and capabilities	Concerned with knowing why things occur; disapproves of lies made with intent to deceive Makes closer peer friendships (boys in larger groups, girls in small groups); enjoys organized clubs Persistent, self-absorbed in school activities; academic performance very important Time concepts can be understood	Likes almost everyone in family Sex differences in interests emerging More contented with world Interest in pleasure leads to hedonistic attitudes toward right and wrong
11	New doubts and tensions Sensitive and full of self-doubts No longer at ease with self and others	High physical activity Big appetite; intense curiosity Enjoys school Has responsible work habits	Challenges parents and all adults Conflicts with siblings Increasing interest in peer friendships away from the family

Table 9.1 (cont.)

Pre-Adolescence

Age (Yrs.)	Self-Concepts	Expected Behaviors	Interests and Social and Family Relationships
12	Doubts and tensions increase in relation to physical changes associated with pubescence	Judgments of right and wrong made increasingly on basis of what others want Often has difficulty in sustaining interest in school work; School grades may fall Chief fears become losing close friends and failing at school Beginning of ability to think some problems through without need of concrete objects	Increasing unhappiness with relationships within the family and with all positions of authority Increasing concern with conformity to peer behavior; increasing disregard of parental norms Increased sensitivity plays role in parent-child conflicts
13	Embarrassment and shyness regarding physiological changes that are taking place Increasing concern with self-concept and with defining identity; Self-esteem tied to academic abilities and school success	Restlessness Masturbation occurs for many Increased interests in friends as source of security Moral decisions often based on what others think Increasing capacity to think abstractly	Increased conflict within family; concern for conformity and popularity Interest in exploring new sexual urges Parents' control of behavior decreases dramatically as new opportunities for outside activities increase

Early Adolescence			
14	Difficulty in being consistent in view of self	Increasing anger and frustration Exploration with peers of many available socially unacceptable things now possible, such as drugs and alcohol Tends to try to make decisions on basis of duty and ethical considerations.	Increasing desire to develop idealistic solutions to problems and to search for consistency in arguments Anger develops toward parents when inconsistencies in parental behavior are noted Experimentation with heterosexual activity may occur
15	Fluctuating self-identity continues Increased introversion	Interest in appearance; girls spend a lot of time combing hair and studying dress styles Many adolescents keep diaries that attest to feelings of self-importance and concern for conformity to group School work continues to slide Experimentation with sexual intercourse may occur	Family disagreements center on sexual interests and activities; exploration of socially unacceptable alcohol and drugs; freedom and responsibility Continuing need to conform to peers

Table 9.1 (cont.)

Age (Yrs.)	Self-Concepts	Expected Behaviors	Interests and Social and Family Relationships
Later Adolescence			
16	Concerns and self-doubt revolve around interest in role identity and future roles in life	Interest in possible future role identities increases interest in academic matters Concern for peer relationships and identity problems still interfere with achievement	Increasing ability to think logically often begins to decrease inconsistency in expectations toward family members
17 and older	Beginning to resolve problem of self-identity although there is still a great deal of self-doubt Gradual development of definitions of self and future	Makes some decisions because of necessity of deciding what to do following completion of high school	Increasing interest in self and future possibilities and relationships Gradually decreasing interest in family relationships except as regards unresolved conflicts

*The material used in this table comes from the following sources: Elkind, D. *A Sympathetic Understanding of the Child Six to Sixteen* (Boston: Allyn & Bacon, 1971); Gibson, J. *Growing Up: A Study of Children* (Reading, Mass.: Addison-Wesley, 1978); and Gibson, J. *Living: A Study of Human Development Throughout the Lifespan* (Reading, Mass.: Addison-Wesley, 1983).

needs. He will not be able yet to talk with you about yours, however. He will also not be able to understand why his parents feel that certain behaviors—as, for example, hitting his younger sister—are bad. At this stage of development, the child understands only that the environment is there for him. Later thinking, language, and other behaviors will change drastically.

Children demonstrate individual differences in the rates at which they go through each stage of development. For this reason, the ages listed in Table 9.1 should be considered as tentative guidelines for what to expect rather than rigid age-determined characteristics. And finally, only a bare minimum of detail can be given in a table that describes development from the preschool years through adolescence. Parents who want to learn more about child development and specific behaviors that can be expected at various stages should refer to one of the texts on this topic listed in Chapter 10.

AGE-RELATED BEHAVIOR DISORDERS THAT REQUIRE PROFESSIONAL HELP

Discipline Is Not a Dirty Word! deals with behaviors that parents often want to teach as well as behaviors that parents want to stop. Most of the behaviors discussed in this book can be dealt with by the discipline methods described here. Some behaviors, however, are important symptoms of more serious problems that may require the assistance of professionals. Table 9.2 includes behaviors symptomatic of some of the more serious disorders. They are described here so that parents can recognize them and seek professional help. Each behavior is listed together with the age at which it is usually first recognized. This list is not complete by any means; parents should remember that whenever they cannot control their children's behavior, it's time to get outside help.

Table 9.2 THE DEVELOPMENT OF AGE-RELATED BEHAVIOR DISORDERS THAT REQUIRE PROFESSIONAL TREATMENT

Age at Which Symptoms Often First Appear	Disorder	Characteristics	Treatment
Preschool years	Autism	Extreme withdrawal and avoidance of contact with others Unresponsiveness often noted in first year of life while infant is being held and fed Histories of crying day and night in infancy Older autistic children exhibit repetitive behaviors such as head knocking, do not speak, and appear uninterested in world	One of the most successful treatments is professional behavior management
Preschool years	Hyperactivity	Extremely high activity levels Inability to pay attention or relax Impulsivity and aggressive behavior, often with temper tantrums Antisocial behaviors such as lying, stealing, or cruelty to animals not uncommon	Some researchers have indicated that diet is related to hyperactivity; some therapists use a variety of techniques, including breathing techniques and methods of improving body control
Preschool years	Long-term regressive behavior	Childish behaviors such as bedwetting or wetting pants long after toilet training has taken place or after the	Love and attention helps Professional therapists use a variety of techniques if regression persists

		child originally outgrew the behavior Occurs frequently after major traumas	
Middle childhood	Childhood schizophrenia	Many symptoms occur, including extremes of activity, sudden mood changes, verbal disturbances, regression, or apathy.	In severe cases, many therapists remove the child from the family to provide full-time therapy
Middle childhood	Deep depression and withdrawal	Persistent feelings of sadness accompanied by quiet behavior Eventual psychological retreat from others Daydreaming, excessive fantasizing Tension and anxiety, accompanied by hypochondriacal symptoms	Behavior management therapy sometimes used successfully Group-centered therapy often effective
Middle childhood	Learning disabilities	Difficulty in school learning even when ability is average or above average May include poor ability to combine vision and movement, poor listening ability, poor grasp of sequence and rhythm, and difficulty in processing several sensory channels simultaneously Often causes confusion of concepts, poor memory, and poor motor coordination	Successful treatment requires early detection with help tailored to each individual child Small-group learning that provides small learning steps and a great deal of reward is often the most successful
Adolescence	Suicidal tendencies	Preceded often but not always by	Identification as soon as these symp-

Table 9.2 (cont.)

Age at Which Symptoms Often First Appear	Disorder	Characteristics	Treatment
		depression and withdrawal at earlier ages	toms appear is important
			Individual and group therapies have been used successfully
		Feelings of accompanying sadness, loneliness or loss; unspecified feelings of "being bad"; negative self-esteem; feelings of being unable to help others; inability to be liked; expectation of being used by others; feelings that the situation won't change—of being wicked, hated, and justly punished	Family therapy also is being used increasingly often with success
		Some of these symptoms occur for most adolescents; when they are frequent and more severe, the likelihood of self-destructive behavior increases	
		Sometimes has not learned to express feelings of anger; often shy, with feelings of anomie, or separation from the rest of society	
Adolescence	Alcoholism and drug addiction	Addiction is preceded by experimentation	Therapy involves providing help to deal with the emotional problems that led to the addiction before the
		The usual alcoholic or drug addict is	

			addiction itself can be handled
		male, quiet, easily influenced, and withdrawn; usually has few friends	
		With addiction, withdrawal and alienation increase	
Adolescence	Delinquency; out-of-control behaviors	Status offenses, vandalism most common	Once a crime has been committed, the problem is dealt with by the legal authorities rather than parents or psychologists
		Increases in incidence of serious crime such as burglary, mugging, and shooting	Many programs use behavior management techniques; group therapy often used in rehabilitation centers
		Frequent history of uncontrollable hostility	
Adolescence	Anorexia nervosa and bulimarexia	Anorexia nervosa, a serious and spreading disorder in this country, involves pathological loss of appetite accompanied by deficiency symptoms and emaciation	Treatment in clinics and hospitals provides medical care as well as psychotherapy to deal with the anger, frustration, and loneliness that, in many cases, have brought on the disorder
		Under pressure from parents, girls may eat, then regurgitate	
		Syndrome begins with belief that eating isn't good, regurgitating begins secretly; severe cases that go untreated may lead to death	
		Bulimarexia involves forced vomiting interspersed with massive overeating	
		Affects more females than males	

CHAPTER 10

Additional Assistance: Useful Reading and Places to Go for Help

USEFUL READING

On Child-Rearing in America: Parenting and Discipline Techniques

Atkin, E., and Rubin, E. *Part-Time Father: A Guide for the Divorced Father.* New York: Vanguard Press, 1976.

Concerned primarily with the difficulties that fathers face in becoming "absent" fathers following divorce; also deals with part-time fathers' subsequent relationships with their children.

Becker, W. *Parents Are Teachers: A Child Management Program.* Champaign, Ill.: Research Press, 1976.

Provides practical information for the parent who wants to turn the home into an environment supportive of educational and social growth.

Biller, H., and Meredith, D. *Father Power.* New York: McKay, 1976.

A how-to-do-it book especially for fathers dealing with ways to handle day-to-day discipline situations when there is no mother in the house to help and when two parents are raising children.

Comer, J., and Pouissant, A. *Black Child Care.* New York: Simon & Schuster, 1975.

Black child care and child development is discussed by two psychiatrists. Extremely useful for parents of black children who want to respond sensitively to their children's interests and concerns.

Carro, G. "The wage-earning mother—what working means to her marriage, her kids—her life. *Ladies Home Journal,* December 1978, pp. 56–59.

A brief description of a study done by the *Ladies Home Journal* that describes national trends in working marriages with children.

Curtis, J. *Working Mothers.* Garden City, N.Y.: Doubleday, 1976.

Very readable interviews with two hundred American women, men, and children; results confirm that U.S. family patterns are in a state of change.

Felker, D. *Building Positive Self-Concepts.* Minneapolis: Burgess, 1974.

A how-to-do-it book that deals primarily with the development of self-esteem in young children and considers other behaviors associated with self-esteem.

Ginott, H. *Between Parent and Child.* New York: Macmillan, 1965.

A classic that all parents should read. Ginott uses examples to show parents how to help relate to their children and how to help children relate to them.

Ginott, H. *Between Parent and Teenager.* New York: Macmillan, 1969.

A follow-up by the author of *Between Parent and Child* designed to deal with the issues of adolescence.

Gordon, T. *P.E.T.: Parent Effectiveness Training.* New York: New American Library, 1970.

A program for teaching parents to listen and to communicate their understanding of what their child is telling them.

Hope, K., and Young, H., eds. *Momma: The Sourcebook for Single Mothers.* New York: New American Library, 1976.

A series of short but useful articles dealing with issues related to handling divorce and problems of working mothers.

Isaacs, S. *The Nursery Years.* New York: Schocken Books, 1968.

A popular manual for parents that describes how to maintain a democratic style of discipline, and, at the same time, set guidelines for what is and is not appropriate behavior; Isaacs is a firm believer in teaching children how to use freedom and choice as well as to be obedient.

Keniston, K., et al. *All Our Children: The American Family Under Pressure,* New York: Harcourt Brace Jovanovich, 1977.

Discusses the problems of parenting and sibling relationships in the American Family today.

LeMasters, E. *Parents in Modern America.* Homewood, Ill.: Dorsey Press, 1977.

Focuses on what is happening to parents who are raising children in America; discusses the particular effects of social changes in the past decade.

Lynn, D. *Daughters and Parents: Past, Present, and Future.* Monterey, Cal.: Brooks/Cole, 1979.

Lynn, D. *The Father: His Role in Child Development,* Monterey, Cal.: Brooks/Cole, 1974.

A description of research describing the father's impact on the development of his children.

Olds, S. *The Mother Who Works Outside the Home.* New York: Child Study Press, 1975.

A small book that provides advice on how to make life easier for working mothers.

Robertiello, R. *Hold Them Very Close, Then Let Them Go.* New York: Dial Press, 1976.

A short primer for parents written by a psychiatrist who views discipline as a very important form of parental love. Many suggestions match closely the findings of Stanley Coopersmith.

Scott, N. *Working Women.* Kansas City, Kan.: Sheed, Andrews & McMeel, 1977.

Examines how women today are coping with the problems of being working mothers in the United States; discusses rearing children as single parents, simultaneously managing home and job responsibilities, and many other topics.

Simon, S., and Olds, B. *Helping Your Child Learn Right from Wrong: A Guide to Values Clarification.* New York: Simon & Schuster, 1976.

A book that explains strategies for parents to use in developing love and friendship in their relations with their children.

Stein, B. *New Parents' Guide to Early Learning.* New York: New American Library, 1976.

Deals with the rearing of infants and very young children; a how-to-do-it book.

On Child and Adolescent Development—for Parents

What to expect at given ages

Goodman, P. *Growing Up Absurd.* New York: Random House, 1960.

> A still-accurate description of adolescence and an excellent social comment on the predicaments that occur to individuals going through this stage of development.

Ilg, F., and Ames, L. *The Gesell Institute's Child Behavior.* New York: Dell, 1959.

> A realistic guide to child behavior in the years from birth to ten; contains a separate section on what to do about discipline.

Spock, B. *Baby and Child Care.* New York: Pocket Books, 1976.

> A classic. This revised edition deals with both development through adolescence and methods of dealing with children.

Scholarly Books and Textbooks on Child and Adolescent Development

Bronfenbrenner, U. *Two Worlds of Childhood.* New York: Russell Sage Foundation, 1970.

> A comparison of child development and family interactions in the U.S. and the U.S.S.R.; the second half of this book contains the author's extremely useful suggestions for correcting problems of child-rearing in this country.

Clarke-Stewart, A. *Child Care in the Family.* New York: Academic Press, 1977.

> A review of research on the effects of early environment on young children, together with advice on a variety of techniques to help facilitate psychological development and provide discipline.

Coopersmith, S. *The Antecedents of Self-Esteem.* San Francisco: Freeman Publishers, 1967.

> An important study for parents to read; describes the variables associated with the development of high, medium, and low self-esteem in a group of young boys; shows clearly the relationship between particular parental behaviors and attitudes and the development of self-esteem.

Gibson, J. *Growing Up: A Study of Children.* Reading, Mass.: Addison-Wesley, 1978.

A comprehensive description of theories of child development, behaviors to expect as children increase in age, and the effects of parental interactions with children on their development.

Gibson, J. *Living: Human Development Through the Lifespan.* Reading, Mass.: Addison-Wesley, 1983.

An extension of *Growing Up: A Study of Children* that describes theories of development throughout the lifespan, as well as behaviors to expect at each age level.

Gibson, J., & Blumberg, P. *Growing Up: Readings on the Study of Children.* Reading, Mass.: Addison-Wesley, 1978.

A series of articles describing children and the ways they interact with their environment at each stage of development from infancy through high school.

Lefrancois, J. *Adolescents.* Belmont, Cal.: Wadsworth, 1976.

A comprehensive description of adolescence.

On Day Care

Daycare in Your Home. HEW Publication No (OHD) 74-217. Washington, D.C.: U.S. Government Printing Office, 1975.

Guidelines for selecting day care; offers advice on what to look for in choosing a day care facility and practical information on what to do when none is available in your community.

Keister, M. *The Good Life for Infants and Toddlers.* New York: Harper & Row, 1970.

Written by the director of a day care facility; a description of the important components of good day care that parents should look for.

Keyserling, M. *Windows on Day Care.* New York: National Council of Jewish Women, 1972.

Describes the variations in the types of day care provided in the U.S. in relation to their effects on the development of preschool children.

On Serious Problem Behaviors of Children and of Parents: Some Guides to Help

Axline, V. *Dibs: In Search of Self.* Boston: Houghton Mifflin, 1964.

A classic case study of a small boy and a description of the approach that helped him solve his emotional problems.

Chapin, W. *Wasted: The Story of My Son's Drug Addiction.* New York: McGraw-Hill, 1972.

A middle-class father describes his son's struggle with marijuana, LSD, and amphetamines and the family's struggle to solve the problem.

Fontana, V. *Somewhere a Child is Crying.* New York: Mentor, 1976.

Describes causes and treatment of child abuse.

Gil, D. *Violence Against Children.* Cambridge, Mass.: Harvard University Press, 1970.

A useful description of just what child abuse is like in this country and what some of the causes are.

Giovannoni, J., and Becerra, R. *Defining Sexual Abuse.* New York: Free Press, 1980.

Points out causes and symptoms of child abuse, what parents should look for, and steps they can take to help alleviate the problems.

Golick, M. *A Parent's Guide to Learning Problems.* Montreal: Association for Children with Learning Disabilities, 1970.

Practical and easy-to-understand advice to help parents teach children with learning problems; contains a series of suggested activities.

Kaufman, B. *Son/Rise.* New York: Harper & Row, 1976.

A book written by the father of an autistic child that describes just what this child and his family went through in working out ways to solve his problem, and the therapy devised by his parents that proved most helpful.

Vine, P. *Families in Pain.* New York: Pantheon, 1982.

A plan to help families of mentally ill children and adults find care from the best possible sources.

SOME PLACES TO BEGIN LOOKING FOR HELP

The following list is not complete, but it provides some sources for parents and children to use as a beginning in their search for help with parenting, discipline, or problem behaviors in the family.

Family and Children's Services

State or federally funded centers. Almost every American city offers state or federally funded services to provide help with parenting, discipline, or problem behaviors in the family. All government-sponsored programs provide a variety of medical and psychological services. Costs vary and usually depend on income. Contact your local center by telephone, explain the problem, and request information concerning what is available in your community. Or contact the U.S. Public Health Service directly.

The federal government provides a manual describing its specific services and ways to contact more than five hundred local mental health centers in this country. (Write for *A Consumer's Guide to Mental Health Services,* DHEW Publication No. ADM 75-214, Rockville, Md: Alcohol, Drug Abuse, and Mental Health Administration, HEW, 1975.)

Other centers providing services in most communities. Many nonprofit agencies, such as the Urban League, the Salvation Army, and the YMCA and YWCA offer family and children's services. Big Brother, a volunteer organization, provides recreation and other service programs for youngsters without fathers. Emergency counseling service for pregnant teenagers is provided in most cities. Check in your yellow pages, and call for specific information.

Crisis Intervention

Many communities in the United States have provided special crisis intervention centers where help can be obtained quickly in emergency situations.

Hotlines. Many communities provide hotline help, where clients can make contact with therapists immediately and anonymously by telephone. Many of these hotlines can be found in the yellow pages of the phone book or in the white pages under the name of the problem leading to the crisis; they provide intervention in emergencies such as potential suicide, child abuse, and drug abuse. The Salvation Army provides a Teen Hotline in many communities for adolescents dealing with all kinds of crises.

The following hotline numbers may be called toll free:

For child abuse: 800-932-0313

For drug emergencies: 800-452-0201

For runaway children: 800-621-4000

If you do not have available to you a hotline for crisis intervention, contact your local family and children's center and ask where to call for help.

Parent Organizations

Many groups have been established throughout the United States by parents concerned with particular problems dealing with parenting, discipline, and problem behaviors in the family. The following organizations have centers in most large cities, and are listed in the telephone book. If you do not have a center in your own community, contact the center nearest you and request information about getting help for your group:

Child Find, Inc. A private clearinghouse for information about missing children with national headquarters in New Platz, N.Y. (Telephone 800-431-5055).

National Federation of Parents for Drug-Free Youth. An organization founded, directed, and administered by parents to educate and assist parents in the prevention and intervention of drug use. (Write to National Headquarters, P.O. Box 722, Silver Spring, Md.)

Parents Anonymous. A parents' organization for mothers and fathers who are child abusers or potential child abusers. This organization provides crisis intervention as well as therapy.

Parents Without Partners. A parents' organization designed to help single parents provide the services they need to raise their children. Parents Without Partners provides information as well as a special organization to help parents meet their own needs as well as those of their children in coping with divorce, widowhood, and single parenting.

Toughlove. An association described in *Time* magazine (June 7, 1982, p. 52) of more than five hundred groups of parents in the U.S. and Canada who have banded together to draw the line and help each other help out-of-control children.

Courses Available in Your Community in Parenting

Credit and noncredit courses are available through your local community colleges and through adult education programs in high schools, colleges, and universities throughout the country. Other places to check for availability of courses include your local church, the Red Cross, the YMCA and YWCA, and Family and Children's Centers.

A NOTE TO READERS: SOME ADDITIONAL INFORMATION

If you are aware of a useful organization not listed here that you think should be included, please send the name and address to me so that I may keep it in my files. I will be glad to send updated listings of places to go for help to readers who send me a self-addressed stamped envelope. Thank you.

Dr. Janice T. Gibson
Department of Educational and Developmental Psychology
Forbes Quadrangle
University of Pittsburgh
Pittsburgh, PA 15260

FOOTNOTES

Chapter 1

1. Stanley Coopersmith's article, "Studies in self-esteem," *Scientific American,* February 1968, pp. 96–100, is a classic and provides an extremely useful model for parents to follow in developing feelings of self-worth in their children.
2. Excellent documentation is provided by R. Winett and R. Winkler in "Current Behavior Modification Programs in the Classroom: Be still, be quiet, be docile," *Journal of Applied Behavioral Analysis,* 1972, no. 5, pp. 499–504.
3. These facts are documented in J. Gibson, *Living: Human Development Through the Lifespan* (Reading, Mass: Addison-Wesley, 1983).

Chapter 2

1. See T.G.R. Bower, *The Perceptual World of the Child* (Cambridge, Mass: Harvard University Press, 1977).
2. The roles of imitation and attachment are discussed in J. Gibson, *Growing Up: A Study of Children* (Reading, Mass: Addison-Wesley, 1981).
3. See J. Gibson, *Living: Human Development Through the Lifespan.*
4. This material is discussed by R. Sprinthall and N. Sprinthall in *Educational Psychology: A Developmental Approach* (Reading, Mass: Addison-Wesley, 1981).
5. This reference comes from Keniston's article, "In Abdicating American Parents," *Newsweek,* September 22, 1975, p. 55.

Chapter 3

1. See W. Friedman, "The Development of Children's Understanding of Cyclic Aspects of Time," *Child Development,* 1977, no. 48, pp. 1593–1599.
2. For a complete discussion of how punishment works, see J. Gibson, *Psychology for the Classroom* (Englewood-Cliffs, N.J.: Prentice-Hall, 1981).

Chapter 4

1. See A. Maslow, *Motivation and Personality* (New York: Harper & Row, 1954). Another source for Maslow's theory is his article, "A Theory of Human Motivation," published in *Psychological Review,* 1943, no. 50, pp. 370–396.
2. Stanley Coopersmith's important work is described in his book, *The Antecedents of Self-Esteem,* (San Francisco: Freeman Press, 1967).
3. See Carl Rogers's classic work, *On Becoming a Person: A Therapist's View of Psychotherapy,* (N.Y.: Houghton Mifflin, 1970).

Chapter 5

1. See S. Freud, "Three essays on the theory of sexuality," in *The Complete Psychology Works of Sigmund Freud, Standard Edition* (London: Hogarth Press, 1905). Diepold and Young discuss the common occurrence of masturbation among American youth in "Empirical studies of adolescent sexual behavior: A critical review," *Adolescence,* Spring 1979, XIV, 53, pp. 45–65.
2. Parents' attitudes and children's behavior are both strongly affected by whether or not parents are comfortable with working away from home. See S. Cohen, "Maternal Employment and Mother-Child Interaction, *Merrill-Palmer Quarterly,* 1978, 24, 3, pp. 189–197.
3. See Erikson's classic book, *Childhood and Society* (2d ed, New York: Norton, 1963).
4. A good source to examine for effects of TV watching is S. Burton, J. Calonico, and D. McSeveney, "Effects of Preschool Television Watching on First Grade Children," *Journal of Communication,* 1978, 29, pp. 164–170.

Chapter 6

1. P. Glick and A. Norton ["Marrying, Divorcing, and Living Together in the U.S. Today", *Population Bulletin,* Washington, D.C.: Population Reference Bureau, 1977, 32(5)] provide interesting statistics concerning the American divorce rate. Many pressures have been cited as the cause of this problem. Journalists point to the high cost of living and other economic pressures, drug and alcohol abuse, and a decline of moral standards. See "A family meeting turns into a feud," *Newsweek,* June 16, 1980, p. 31.
2. This extensive work was done by J. Wallerstein and J. Kelly. Two useful works for parents are *Surviving the Breakup: How Children Actually Cope with Divorce* (New York: Basic Books, 1980); and "Divorce and

Children" in J. Noshpitz (ed.), *Basic Handbook of Child Psychiatry,* 1979, 4, pp. 339–346.

3. Sours describes this problem in some detail in his article, "Enuresis," which appears in B. Wolman, J. Egan, and A. Ross (eds.), *Handbook of Treatment of Mental Disorders in Childhood and Adolescence* (Englewood Cliffs, N.J.: Prentice-Hall, 1978), pp. 153–160.
4. These data were taken from the U.S. Bureau of the Census, 1980.
5. Flextime is described in an interesting article by Betty Friedan, "Feminism Takes a New Turn," in *New York Times Magazine,* November 18, 1979, pp. 40–106.
6. John Bowlby points out that baby sitters can serve as secondary attachment figures for infants. See Bowlby's article, "The Nature of the Child's Tie to His Mother," *International Journal of Psychoanalysis,* 1958, 39, pp. 1–34.

Chapter 7

1. See Chapter 14 in J. Gibson, *Growing Up: A Study of Children.*
2. Chapter 9 in J. Gibson, *Growing Up: A Study of Children* describes this period. Erik Erikson may be the best-known psychoanalyst to deal with this topic. See his book, *Childhood and Society* (New York: Norton, 1950) for a detailed description.
3. See P. Richards, "Middle-Class Vandalism and Age-Status Conflict," *Social Problems,* April 1979, 26(4), pp. 482–497.
4. Truancy often is the result of dissatisfaction with achievement, feelings of uselessness, and the desire to get relief from what are felt to be unbearable conditions. See J. Gibson, *Growing Up: A Study of Children.*
5. A good source of information on drugs and drug abuse is *Resource Book for Drug Abuse Education* (Washington, D.C.: U.S. Department of H.E.W., National Clearinghouse for Mental Health Information, 1979).
6. See D. Lipton, et al., "A Survey of Substance Use Among Junior and Senior High School Students in New York State," *American Journal of Drug Abuse,* 1977, 4(2), pp. 153–164.
7. B. Dykeman gives an excellent list of systems to look for when children try to hide their addiction in his article, "Teenage Alcoholism—Detecting Those Early Warning Signals," *Adolescence,* 1979, XIV, 54, pp. 251–253.
8. There are four useful sources of statistical information on these topics:

(1) J. Diepold and R. Young, "Empirical Studies of Adolescent Sexual Behavior: A Critical Review," *Adolescence,* Spring 1979, XIV, 53, pp. 45–65; (2) J. Hopkins, "Sexual Behavior in Adolescence," *Journal of Social Issues,* 1977, 33, 2, pp. 67–85; (3) B. Rienzo, "The Status of an Education," *Phi Delta Kappan,* November 1981, pp. 192–193; and (4) A. Vener, and C. Stewart, "Adolescent Sexual Behavior in Middle America Revisited," *Journal of Marriage and the Family,* 1974, 36, pp. 728–741.

9. These were reasons given to J. Kantner and H. Zelnik when they interviewed pregnant teenagers. The Kantner and Zelnik study is reported in "Sexual Experience of Young Unmarried Women in the United States," *Family Planning Perspectives,* 1972, 4, pp. 9–18.

Chapter 8

1. These statistical data were derived from the following sources: (1) "Child Abuse Called National Epidemic," *American Psychological Association Monitor,* Winter 1979, p. 1; (2) S. Cohen and A. Sussman, "The Incidence of Child Abuse in the United States," *Child Welfare,* 1975, 54, pp. 432–443; (3) W. Farmer, "No Paddle Bawl in Sweden," *Parade,* March 16, 1980, pp. 24–26; (4) J. Garbarino and A. Crouter, "Defining the Community Context for Parent-Child Relations: The Correlate of Child Maltreatment," *Child Development,* 1978, 49, pp. 604–616.

2. Studies documenting these conclusions include the following: (1) B. Melnick, and J. Hurley, "Distinctive Personality Attributes of Child-Abusing Mothers," *Journal of Consulting and Clinical Psychology,* 1969, 33, pp. 746–749; (2) J. Spinetta and D. Rigler, "The Child-Abusing Parent: A Psychological Review," *Psychological Bulletin,* 1972, 77, 4, pp. 296–304.

3. J. Giovannoni and R. Becerra discuss this syndrome in their book, *Defining Sexual Abuse* (New York: Free Press, 1980). A. Green provides additional data on the same problem in his article, "Child Abuse," in G. Wolman, J. Egan, and A. Ross (eds.), *Handbook of Treatment of Mental Disorders in Childhood and Adolescence* (Englewood Cliffs, N.J.: Prentice-Hall, 1978).

4. See S. Sgroi's article, "Kids with Clap: Gonorrhea as an Indicator of Child Sexual Assault," in *Victimology,* 1977, 2, 2, pp. 251–267.

5. This information has been adapted from *The Harvard Medical School Health Letter,* March 1981, p. 3.

Author Index

Topical Index